# The Great Deception

# THE GREAT DECEPTION

## The Inside Story of How the Kremlin Took Over Cuba

JAMES MONAHAN AND
KENNETH O. GILMORE

Farrar, Straus and Company · New York

*Portions of this book appeared originally in the January 1963* Reader's Digest *and are included here by permission of the editors of the* Digest.

Library of Congress catalog card number 63–12491
First Printing, 1963
Published simultaneously in Canada by
Ambassador Books, Ltd., Toronto
Manufactured in the United States of America
Printed by American Book–Stratford Press, Inc.

# Contents


| | | |
|---|---|---|
| FOREWORD | | vii |
| PART ONE | The False Dawn | 1 |
| PART TWO | Temple or Tomb? | 23 |
| PART THREE | The Awakening | 53 |
| PART FOUR | Dismal Springtime | 97 |
| PART FIVE | Darkness Descends | 123 |
| PART SIX | Exporting the Revolution | 151 |
| PART SEVEN | The Kremlin-West | 181 |

# Foreword

This book is the outgrowth of a project which began early in 1962 when the editors of the *Reader's Digest* asked one of the authors (JM) to make a preliminary study that might answer the following questions:

1. Is there need for a book which will provide a straightforward, factual account of what really happened in Cuba between January 1, 1959, and the present, told entirely from the Cuban viewpoint?

2. Can such a first-hand account be compiled from detailed and preferably tape-recorded interviews with a large and representative number of Cubans, perhaps several hundred, who will give their individual views, attitudes and experiences during this period?

3. Can we avoid the pitfalls that are likely to occur in any "random sample" of Cubans-in-exile by selecting interviewees in a way to insure the inclusion of (a) all age groups, (b) economic and social classes, (c) occupations and professions, (d) political opinions, and (e) geographic locations within Cuba? Can we establish, by the same preselection, the veracity and trustworthiness of those who speak for the record?

4. Finally, is it possible to reach reliable sources within Cuba for the purpose of verifying and perhaps elaborating the material obtained in interviews and to bring these accounts abreast of developments within Cuba today?

To provide the answers to these questions we had the invaluable assistance of the editors of *Selecciones,* the Spanish-language edition of the *Digest,* and staff members located throughout Latin America. We also obtained the advice and guidance of a small and carefully selected group of Cubans who subsequently served as advisors until the main project was completed.

Work on the project itself began in March. In the months that followed, several hundred Cubans were interviewed, and the conversations recorded, in individual sessions which seldom lasted less than two hours and often continued over several days. The list of interviewees was constantly expanding; a single interview, for example, would reveal things which pointed to the necessity of talking to two or more people who had participated in the same incident or development, or who were present in the same town or province at the same time. Meanwhile, hundreds of pages of transcribed material were being studied and coordinated; this also revealed discrepancies and blank spots which required additional questioning or interviews with new people.

For safety's sake, we operated from the beginning on the assumption that, sooner or later, the authorities in Castro's Cuba would learn about the project. Early in June, this assumption was proved correct. We received reports from friends in Puerto Rico, Mexico, Venezuela—and even one from Havana—that on June 1, 1962, Radio Havana had broadcast an hour-long diatribe against *Selecciones* and the *Digest.* The most interesting disclosure in the broadcast was a tacit admission that *Selecciones* was still being read inside Cuba. The broadcaster ridiculed the *Digest* articles dealing with life in Red

China, Southeast Asia and the Soviet-bloc countries and particularly the disclosures by defected Communists and refugees. "Here we read the same kind of stories," the broadcaster stated, "but by an author with a name like Gonzalez or Perez who escapes by sea instead of crossing Iron or Bamboo curtains. Now these terrible things happen in Cuba, according to *Selecciones*. Here we read *Selecciones,* but now there exists a difference. We know what is happening in Cuba, and we can judge to what degree that magazine has always lied. . . ."

Our Latin American informants attached particular significance to this broadcast. "They know what you are up to," wrote a friend in Caracas. "But they obviously do not know when or how soon you will publish. This broadcast, we are convinced, is merely a preliminary build-up for the real attack which will follow the publication of your report."

We had assured the Cubans who supplied us with information that their identities would be disclosed only with their specific permission. After finishing this book, the reader will understand why many individuals asked that a pseudonym or cover-name be used and, perhaps, that certain identifying details be altered or omitted in order to protect relatives who still were within the reach of Castro's G-2. However, there were some instances in which no name-changing or alterations (short of fiction) could disguise an individual who played a prominent role in a specific situation. The alternatives, then, were to use the real name and actual facts or to eliminate the material entirely. We admire those who, faced with the problem, told us simply, "Go ahead and use my name."

We wish it were possible to acknowledge, in full detail, the close and fruitful contacts which were established with people still living in Castro's Cuba. They not only enabled us to verify material but added many revealing and timely details to the report itself. For obvious reasons, that story must be withheld until a happier time.

Space does not permit us to name all those to whom we are indebted for the parts they played in making this book possible; but, with a few exceptions, we have been able to thank them individually. We would be remiss, however, if we failed to give special commendation to Miss Elinor Griest of the *Digest* editorial staff, our chief interviewer and investigator, who also served as captain and coordinator of the team when both of us had to be away from the home base for days and weeks at a time.

James Monahan
Kenneth O. Gilmore

# Part One

# THE FALSE DAWN

Toward midnight on December 31, 1958, the island of Cuba, which traditionally lighted up the Caribbean skies with celebrations on New Year's Eve, lay under a pall of gloom. The provinces of Las Villas, Camagüey and Oriente were paralyzed by the spreading conflict between Fidel Castro's rebels and the larger, better armed, but dispirited troops of the dictator, Fulgencio Batista. Matanzas, east of Havana, lay directly in the course of the onrushing revolution. There was sporadic fighting in the western province of Pinar del Río, and within the preceding twenty-four hours Havana itself had been panicked by gunfire and rocked by explosions set off by rebel saboteurs.

"Cubans could see nothing happy in the New Year," says Luis Manrara, a Havana businessman who later became head of the Truth About Cuba Committee. "There was the prospect only of a bloody civil war. Most of us went to bed that night with a prayer on our lips and with fear in our hearts."

Father Armando Llorente, a Jesuit priest who once was Fidel Castro's close friend and spiritual advisor at the Colegio de Belén, finished reading his Divine Office and put aside his breviary with a worried frown. A fortnight earlier he had made a hazardous journey up into the Sierra Maestra to visit his erstwhile pupil who soon might hold the destiny of Cuba in his hands. "Among other things, Fidel had told me that it might be another six months before he got control of Oriente province," says Father Llorente, "and perhaps ten months before the last Batista garrison in Cuba was subdued. I returned to Havana convinced that Fidel's 'total war against the tyranny' would be long and bloody."

Señor Alonso León, sales supervisor of a large soap company, took a last look at the locked doors of the two-car garage behind his home in a suburb of Havana. Hidden in the false bottom of his blue 1958 Chevrolet were guns, ammunition, and enough TNT to blow up the entire neighborhood. On New Year's Day he intended to put his wife, mother-in-law and four children into that car and drive to Pinar del Río, ostensibly to visit his ninety-one-year-old grandmother, but actually to deliver the "goods" to the rebels who were operating from hideouts in the Sierra de los Organos.

Samuel Nodarse, known as Flavio in the underground, sat beside the window of a darkened, sparsely furnished cottage in Varadero Beach, listening to the music and wild laughter in the adjoining cottage owned by the chief of police. For the past month orders had been out to bring in Flavio dead or alive. Hence, Nodarse had spent his days slipping through the police dragnet, and his nights in different hideouts provided by the underground. On New Year's Eve he reached Varadero Beach and had contacted fat, taciturn Benito Valdés, the local grocer. "Get into my truck," Valdés had told him. "I am about to deliver the refreshments for the Chief's orgy, and there is a vacant house next door. Who would look for Flavio right under the Chief's drunken nose?"

Angel Lastra, a twenty-seven-year-old cane-cutter, said goodbye to his young wife and three children in the mid-island city of Sancti Spíritus, which had been captured by the rebels on Christmas Day, and went to join the column commanded by Ché Guevara near Santa Clara. On the way he stopped to pick up his pal, Paco Alvarez, and found him lying asleep amidst a clutter of empty beer bottles. Paco muttered an obscenity on all revolutions and lapsed back into his stupor; Angel Lastra took the dark, dangerous road to Santa Clara alone.

In Santiago de Cuba Señora Pilar Quintero, a short, stout dark-haired woman, known in the Sierra Maestra as the "Good Angel of the Underground" because of the miracles she performed in getting food and medicines to the rebel army, said a prayer for her four sons and daughters and their nineteen children, and asked God to look mercifully upon all Cubans in the dark days ahead. "I knew that Fidel planned to take Santiago," she says, "and I knew that Batista's planes would destroy us before he allowed our great city to be taken by the rebels."

### *The Incredible Bolo*

At his home in the Vedado section of Havana, Señor Ernesto Santamarina, a middle-class businessman, lay sleepless with an incredible *bolo* (rumor) nagging at his mind. On Tuesday, December 30, the head of a Havana travel agency had told him that hotel suites had been leased in New York and Miami for the young Batistas and their families. Then, that very day, his cousin, who worked in the special passport section of the Ministry of Foreign Relations, had given some credence to the story. Her office, she said, had been busy for days renewing and validating passports not only for the Batistas but for many high officials in the government. Ernesto decided this could mean only one thing: the dictator was getting ready to quit Cuba.

At dinner on New Year's Eve he had told his story to the family and a few old friends. Everyone laughed at him ("the only good laugh of the evening") and called him naive, gullible, even an old fool. "Don't make yourself ridiculous, Ernesto," his brother Ignacio scolded. "You know Batista will never give up that easily. He will give Cuba a blood bath before he lets Castro's rebels take over."

Ernesto shrugged and said no more. But he was unable to dismiss the possibility from his mind.

He was still wide awake at 2:15 A.M., when he heard planes from nearby Camp Columbia roaring overhead. He called to his wife: "Listen! Since when have we heard planes leaving Columbia at this hour of the morning? I tell you those reports are true!"

Moments later, while he was turning the radio dial, the telephone rang. It was his brother. "You were right, Ernesto! The tyrant is gone. I have just had a call from our neighbor whose son is at Camp Columbia. He says the airport now is jammed with Batistianos trying to leave the country before the rebels can get them. Pass the good news."

Ernesto began dialing numbers. Every line was busy. Then, between calls, his own phone rang again, and it was his old friend, Professor Betancourt, who had been at dinner that night. "Forgive me for doubting you, old friend. But apologies can wait. This is wonderful news. Cuba is free. There will be no more bloodshed. Now Fidel Castro can take over."

"So?" Ernesto sounded skeptical. "Are you sure that is good? Can this fellow be trusted?"

"You doubt him? Please, Ernesto, do not force me to call you a fool again. Fidel Castro is our liberator, a man sent by Divine Providence at this crucial hour. He asks nothing for himself—you have heard him. He wants Cuba's freedom. Now, you must excuse me—I have other calls to make."

Ernesto Santamarina recalls: "I sat there thinking. Why *not* Fidel? Who else was there? What did I have against him? Nothing—except the doubts of a man who has lived long enough to be leery of all politicians. Fidel was a zealot, a rabble rouser, and a radical. But I didn't believe he was a Communist—that was typical Batista propaganda. What chance would a Communist have in Cuba? So, like the vast majority of Cubans, I decided that I was for Fidel, and immediately I felt better. In my case, the spell must have lasted for at least sixty days!"

By noontime on New Year's Day the glad tidings had spread throughout Cuba. From his command post near Palma Soriano in the Sierra Maestra, Fidel Castro had broadcast a warning: The war was not over. The revolution would go on until the last Batista garrison had surrendered. There would be a nationwide general strike until the new provisional government was established. Nonetheless everyone knew that the struggle was over.

Alonso León never made the trip to Pinar del Río: he spent New Year's Day tearing out the false bottom and removing the secret compartments from his blue Chevrolet. Henceforth, he decided happily, the trunk compartment would hold only picnic baskets, vacation luggage and, of course, the sample cases of the business he had been neglecting. "I never dreamed," he says, "that before the year was over that same Chevy would be running arms for an entirely different underground."

Benito Valdés, the grocer, burst into Samuel Nodarse's hideout with a loud whoop and tore the sheets from the bed. "Wake up and celebrate, Flavio," he shouted, waving a bottle of wine. "The tyrant is gone. The revolution is over. We have no more need for hideouts. Drink, Flavio, drink!" Nodarse rubbed the sleep from his eyes; when he was sure that Valdés was neither drunk nor mad, he refused the wine and said he must hurry to his home in Matanzas. He wanted to see his wife and their new baby. He had already chosen his son's name—William Fidel.

Young Angel Lastra heard the news in Santa Clara in mid-morning. The war was over, there was no more need for fighting men, so he turned around and headed back to Sancti Spíritus. Now, he told himself, he could raise his family decently and in peace, working the land that Fidel Castro had promised to every peasant. Hours later, on the streets of Sancti Spíritus, he met Paco Alvarez, red-eyed and hung over, but in high spirits, and now wearing the black-and-red armband of the 26th of July Movement and toting a tommy gun. Paco greeted him with a mock salute: "Well, Chico, so you have come home from the wars! Listen, amigo, while I tell you something. Fidel can keep his land! Who wants to grub for a living? Not Paco!" He hefted the gun and threw out his chest. "Being a soldier is much better, no?"

Pilar Quintero's household had been in a whirlwind ever since the news arrived, officially, from the 26th of July headquarters. Fidel Castro would be in Santiago that night; an official reception was to be held at the city hall, and Señora Quintero was expected. Her daughters, her sons' wives, even her favorite grandchild, Gracia, had wailed that Pilar didn't have a decent thing to wear. Then they had set to work cleaning, mending, pressing a faded black taffeta dress which she wore only to funerals. "I will wear only what I have on," Pilar declared. "Otherwise Fidel might not recognize me! But then he may not know me at all any more. Why should he? Fidel Castro, may God bless him, now stands with the immortals of Cuban history!"

Father Llorente had heard the news shortly after dawn, and had offered the first Mass of the New Year for the special intention of Fidel Castro, now a man desperately in need of Divine grace and guidance. "Fidel was no longer a Catholic," says Father Llorente. "I knew he was an apostate, even a man who scoffed at God. He was surrounded by men whose hearts and minds were filled with evil. But I was convinced that Fidel himself was not a Communist. He had assured me of that himself. So, with God's grace, perhaps there was still time to save Fidel—and Cuba."

## Liberator and Savior

The streets of Santiago de Cuba, "cradle of the revolution," were jammed with joyous, cheering men, women and children late on New Year's night when Fidel Castro entered the city leading his column of bearded warriors, and marched directly to the Moncada Barracks where, on July 26, 1953, he had staged the reckless but dramatic attack which gave his 26th of July Movement its name. Now he accepted the garrison's surrender without ceremony. Then he went to the studios of Radio CMKC whose co-owner, José Manuel Berenguer, an old friend and leader of the 26th of July Movement, was waiting for him.

"Fidel had sent word earlier," says Berenguer, "telling me to make arrangements for the victory speech he intended to make that night in Céspedes Park. He arrived at the studio about eleven o'clock, looking very tired, yet bursting with enthusiasm and nervous energy, and talking without even a pause. 'Tonight,' he said, 'I will proclaim Santiago de Cuba the new capital.'

"Several times before Fidel had mentioned Santiago as the future capital, but I never took him seriously. Nevertheless Santiago was the most progressive city in Cuba, and we Santiagüeros deeply resented the political power and pre-eminence of Havana. So what Fidel said was music to our ears.

"What I didn't learn until weeks later was that Fidel had serious doubts about Havana's loyalty to the revolution. That was why he had put off his own entry into Havana for a week, and had declared the crippling general strike until rebel troops commanded by Ché Guevara and Camilo Cienfuegos were in control of the city. That was the reason also, as I discovered later, why he wanted me to establish a new radio network based in Oriente province—he knew the Santiagüeros could be trusted."

From CMKC they went to the city hall where the leaders of the 26th of July Movement and the Civic Resistance were waiting to honor the hero of the revolution. Fidel singled out Señora Pilar Quintero and embraced her affectionately. "Pilar, my angel," he said, "I have great plans for you. You are going to fill the bellies of our children and peasants and make them strong as you did my men in the hills."

However, Señor Gerardo Abascal, a loyal revolutionary who had served in the Civic Resistance, thought that Fidel Castro seemed less cordial to the local business and professional men who were his hosts. "He treated us rather coldly," says Abascal. "He kept us at arm's length, talked over our heads, and even turned his back. But, and this made it even worse, there were some people whom he greeted effusively, talked to confidentially and at great length, and kept beside him during the reception. These men had never done anything for the revolution! Several were well-known local Communists whom we despised.

"This made me angry, and I mentioned it to my colleagues. Why was Fidel pushing aside the people who had worked hard and loyally for the revolution, often at the risk of their lives, families and businesses? Why did he favor these opportunists who had done nothing to help him? But my friends wouldn't listen. They said I was imagining things."

Castro made his speech that night to an overflow crowd in Céspedes Park. On the platform beside him were Dr. Manuel Urrutia Lleó, whom Fidel had named the provisional President of Cuba, and Monsignor Enrique Pérez Serantes, Archbishop of Santiago, whose intercession with Batista had saved Castro from the death penalty after the abortive attack on the Moncada Barracks.

"Fidel was in top form that night," Señor Abascal recalls. "He was the liberator, the Christlike savior, modest in victory, shunning all honors, asking nothing for himself, thinking only of Cuba. Again he promised free elections, free speech, free press, land for the landless peasants, and the complete restoration of our democratic Constitution of 1940. He was inspiring and reassuring. The crowd went wild.

"He did get in one jibe, which I felt he meant for us, when he declared that he 'owed nothing to anyone who was not with me in the Sierra.' But my friends didn't get it. When I saw the ecstasy on their faces I said to myself sadly, 'Chico, if you have any doubts or suspicions of Fidel Castro you had better keep them to yourself. No one will listen to you, much less believe what you say!' "

Yet there was one man, lost in the crowd that night, who might have listened to Gerardo Abascal and, indeed, even confirmed Abascal's vague fears. He was a heavy-set young man with dark, blazing eyes, and he wore the tattered uniform of the rebel army. Major Higinio ("Nino") Díaz was an authentic hero of the Sierra Maestra, a fearless guerrilla fighter, and a military leader who had the complete devotion of his men. But he had been stripped of his rank, deprived of his revolutionary honors, and had barely escaped being shot by Raúl Castro's firing squad. His crime: *anti-Communist* activities in the rebel army.

### *What Nino Knew*

Until 1956, Nino Díaz had been a successful coffee buyer, a jovial young fellow who had legions of devoted friends throughout Cuba, which he traveled regularly. But then as he made his rounds he began to hear more and more of the cruelty, torture and even death visited upon Cubans by Batista's tyranny. Nino Díaz simply went on traveling back and forth over Cuba from Oriente to Pinar del Río, but now his coffee-buying was less a profitable business than a convenient cover for his activities in the anti-Batista underground.

Finally, in late 1957, after Fidel Castro had taken his

stand in the Sierra Maestra, Nino Díaz went into the hills and joined the small rebel army. He proved to be a tough fighter with a flair for guerrilla tactics, and a born leader of men. Moreover, he was able to enlist his loyal friends throughout the eastern provinces in the underground movement which supported the rebels in the hills. Soon Nino was promoted to captain and then to major (the highest rank in the rebel army), and his "revolutionary honors" or commendations were envied but respected by most men in the Sierra Maestra.

"My troubles," says Nino Díaz, "began late in the summer of 1958. Carlos Rafael Rodríguez, whom I knew and disliked as the boss of the Cuban Communist Party, came up into the Sierra and made some sort of a pact with Fidel and Raúl. Immediately thereafter his Communist 'recruits' began to come in droves. They were not good soldiers, but it soon became obvious that they weren't supposed to fight. Their job was to spread out among the troops and work as political indoctrinators. With Raúl Castro's permission, they even went out and organized Marxist study groups among the local peasants who were loyal supporters of the revolution.

"When several of these 'commissars' turned up in my troop, I listened to their Communist propaganda, then I kicked them out and told Raúl Castro that if my men were going to be indoctrinated I intended to be the indoctrinator myself. And I did start several anti-Communist study groups with my own men.

"About that time a dozen or so of the Communists confiscated a nearby farm, shooting and killing one of the peasants, and took over the place for themselves. I threw them all into jail, and they stayed there until Raúl Castro released them. Then my real troubles began.

"First, we would discover our rifles jammed, or someone would have tampered with our machine guns. I knew the troublemakers, but I couldn't do anything about them.

They were Raúl's boys. Then Raúl began assigning me to suicidal missions, hoping that I would be killed. Once he ordered me to take twenty men and occupy an exposed position on the outskirts of Santiago and to knock off any reinforcements that were sent out from the Batista garrison. We were ordered to hold that position for ten days. By the end of the fifth day we had run out of ammunition. By Raúl Castro's orders, no more ammunition or supplies were sent to us.

"We divided up into groups of three or four men and made commando raids, seizing Batista's men and taking their arms and ammunition. The local farmers supplied us with food and even volunteered to join our ranks. We finally got back to the base with our mission accomplished and more than twice as many men as we started with.

"Then one of the Communists, whom Raúl had promoted to captain, shot and killed several peasants. I placed him under arrest and took him into our headquarters, and demanded a court martial. Raúl Castro sent word for me to remain there until the court was convened because there were other prisoners to be tried. Then I discovered that I was one of the prisoners.

"The charge was that I had conspired with a former captain in Batista's army, a man I had never seen before we met in court, to kill Fidel. This fellow actually confessed, and gave perjured evidence against me. Raúl Castro himself presided at the trial. I was sent back to my cell, without being allowed to refute the fellow's lies, and there I got the word that I was to face a firing squad on October 20, 1958."

However, Raúl Castro failed to take into consideration the popularity of Nino Díaz. Men threatened to rebel or desert if Nino was shot. Then petitions began to arrive from the peasants. Finally, delegates from underground cells in Oriente, Las Villas and Camagüey came to warn

Fidel and Raúl that if Nino Díaz was executed the effect on the revolution could be disastrous. Thus Nino's sentence was reduced to an indefinite prison term with loss of rank and revolutionary honors.

"The so-called jailors were my friends," says Nino Díaz. "They allowed me every freedom, and I could have escaped at any time. But I knew that if I ran away it might have a bad effect on the people who had interceded for me. They were all loyal Fidelistas, they were unaware of the Communist problem, and they might think that I really was guilty of trying to kill Fidel. So I waited until New Year's morning. Then I knew that Raúl would have me shot anyway, since he now had nothing to lose. I said goodbye to my friends, the jailors, and one of them even provided me with a horse on which I rode into Santiago late on New Year's night."

Nino Díaz remained in Santiago de Cuba during most of January. Through an intermediary Raúl Castro sent word that his rank and honors would be restored if he rejoined the rebel army.

"I refused, of course," says Nino, "because I knew that Raúl would have me shot or thrown into jail. My friends thought I was crazy. They said I was embittered by my experience, and that communism had become an obsession with me. 'Look at the government Fidel has given us,' they said. 'Men like President Urrutia, Rufo López Fresquet, Miró Cardona, Sorí Marín. They are Catholics, moderates, even conservatives. Where are the Communists?' I told them, 'Well, let's see how long these good Catholic moderates remain in the government.' Later, when Urrutia had to seek asylum in an embassy and the rest of his moderates went into exile, these same friends said to me, 'Nino, you are a prophet! We were the crazy ones.' By that time we were working in the new anti-Castro underground."

## *The Ingathering of Comrades*

Dr. Luis Benítez, prominent psychiatrist, remembers driving along the Central Park in Havana one day early in January. "On the front of a building," he says, "we saw a big banner marking the new headquarters of the PSP [Partido Socialista Popular], the Communist Party of Cuba, which was outlawed in 1952. I laughed and told my wife, 'Well, this seems just like old times.'

"Nevertheless, this did give me an uneasy feeling. I had known Fidel while we were in the university and I had disliked him. He was a trouble-maker and a radical, but I didn't think he was a Communist—he just had the 'red measles' which many students had in those days. He later became a political zealot and fanatic, but I thought the experience in the Sierra Maestra had sobered and matured him. The fact that there were Communists in the rebel army, which was well known, didn't bother me.

"Of course, the truth was that, like most Cubans, I *wanted* to believe in Fidel. I had been anti-Batista, I was for the revolution, and I wanted Castro to succeed. So I saw the things in him I wanted to see, and I rejected or denied evidence to the contrary. Self-delusion, unfortunately, is a common indulgence, even among psychiatrists."

Dr. Jorge Castellanos, then professor of history at the University of Oriente, a former member of the Communist Party and for a time an editorial writer for *Hoy*, saw nothing particularly alarming in the bold re-emergence of the PSP.

"I considered this natural and inevitable," he says. "The dictatorship was ended, political freedom was restored, and Communists waste no time in getting back into action. As a matter of fact, in Cuba, they had been active all along, although not openly. While Batista outlawed the party in 1953, after having a close working alliance with it during 1938–1944, he never really persecuted the Communists. Many of the party leaders went into exile after 1953, but others remained quietly in Cuba, and some even held on to the government jobs Batista had given them originally. There was a sort of 'gentlemen's agreement.'

"But the Communists in Cuba were a comparative handful, and the powerful, predominantly anti-Communist 26th of July Movement could have destroyed them or made them politically impotent. That is what Cubans like myself who belonged to the movement expected to happen. But instead Fidel Castro, for reasons of his own, chose to recognize the Communists as a legal party, and then set about deliberately to destroy the 26th of July Movement as a political organ."

Dr. Castellanos grew more concerned as he watched the "ingathering" of the comrades during early 1959. "Thanks to Batista's hypocrisy," he says, "many did not have to travel far. Blas Roca, secretary of the PSP, had spent his years 'underground' in a villa in the Havana suburbs which was owned by Batista's Prime Minister. Carlos Rafael Rodríguez, who came down from the Sierra Maestra with Fidel, had been living in luxury at Boca Ciega beach, and César Escalante had been a guest of Havana's Municipal Nursery No. 5, which was run by his wife. Even the unsavory character, Joaquín Ordoqui, strong-arm man of the PSP, occupied a house in the Vedado section of Havana, from which he managed the distribution of the Communists' clandestine publications.

"But what really astonished me was the sudden influx of the Cuban Communists who had been in exile. For example, one of the first to arrive was the sinister little man, Fabio Grobart, a Pole who was once known as Aron Sinkovitch. Until he went behind the Iron Curtain in 1952, Grobart for years had run a dingy little tailor shop which was a blind for an elaborately furnished Communist 'command post' in the rear. Fabio Grobart was the 'Gray Eminence' of the Cuban party, and the one who really was Moscow's 'Man in Havana.'

"Lázaro Peña, Communist boss of the labor movement during the first Batista regime, returned from Prague via Mexico; Osmani Cienfuegos, Alfredo Guevara, and Emilio Aragonés came from Mexico; and Ramón ('Monguito') Calcines, leader of the Cuba Communist youth movement, arrived from one of his many visits to the Soviet bloc. During 1953–1958 Calcines had traveled back and forth [between Cuba and the Soviet-bloc countries] with Batista's knowledge, and had even attended conferences in Communist China and Outer Mongolia.

"These hard-core Communists were not taken into the government immediately; that was to be done later. Their first assignments were to infiltrate and control the rebel army and the labor unions, and through the unions to prepare for taking over the press, radio, television, public utilities, and finally all Cuban business and industry."

Carlos Lozano, a young medical student serving in the 26th of July Movement, eyewitnessed the Castro regime's first attempt to destroy all traces of its Communist past. "On the night of January 3," he says, "I was on guard duty at the headquarters of BRAC [Bureau for the Repression of Communist Activities]. The building, which contained the government's secret files on Communist activities in Cuba, had been sealed and we had orders not to allow any unauthorized person near the premises. But that night a truckload of rebel army men drove up and the lieutenant showed us orders signed by Major Ché Guevara. The files were removed from the building, loaded on to the truck, and taken to La Cabaña Fortress where, I was told, they were burned."

This unpublicized incident was reported to Salvador Díaz Versón, former chief of the Army Military Intelligence Service, who had resigned in 1952 in protest against

Batista's *coup d'état,* and then had become president of the Cuban Anti-Communist League and editor of the magazine *Occidente.*

"The BRAC files," he contends, "were begun in 1948 under President Prío; the League files dated back to 1928 and were much more complete. We had dossiers on every Communist and crypto-Communist in Cuba, including one on Fidel Castro. That was what worried me particularly when I heard about the BRAC raid.

"A few weeks earlier, on December 14, we had invited some friends and supporters to our headquarters to celebrate the League's thirtieth anniversary. The archives, which were kept in a special, locked room, were of particular interest. Unfortunately, our guests were told specifically about File A-9-43 which contained reports, documents, affidavits and even photographs which established beyond any doubt that Fidel Castro, while not a card-carrying member of the Cuban party, had been actively associated with the international Communist apparatus since 1943.

"While our guests were all anti-Communists and connected with the League in some way, it seemed likely that someone might talk carelessly about the Castro dossier and be overheard by a servant or some stranger. Moreover, the regime and the party undoubtedly knew all about our operations even if they were not aware of the Castro file. But after January 1, 1959, there was no way of removing the archives from the building or finding a safe hiding place for them.

"Three weeks after the BRAC raid, on January 23, several trucks pulled up before the League headquarters. People in the adjoining apartment houses, attracted by the noise, looked out and saw the trucks plainly marked as belonging to the 7th Military District (La Cabaña). They saw the uniformed men enter the building and begin loading the cases on to the trucks. There was nothing stealthy about the operation, which took several hours. Before departing the soldiers even made bonfires in the street with bundles of the magazine, *Occidente,* and several thousand copies of my book, *Red Czarism.*

"Two days later, while I was driving along Fifth Avenue in Havana, my automobile was riddled by machine-gun bullets fired from a passing car. I miraculously escaped being hit, and I drove directly to an embassy where I asked for asylum."

Captain Carlos Rodríguez Quesada, veteran labor leader in the sugar industry, was with the rebel army in the Escambray Mountains in December 1958 when plans were unveiled for the Communist infiltration of the Cuban labor movement.

"Ché Guevara called a meeting of labor leaders which I attended," he says. "He told us that we had to agree upon a seven-member committee which would take over the CTC [Cuban Confederation of Workers] as soon as the revolution ended. The slate he had drawn up contained a number of suspicious characters two of whom, Ursinio Rojas of the sugar workers, and Vicente Pérez of the tobacco workers, were well-known Communist agitators in the labor movement. There was a big argument because many of us did not want to have organized labor again under Communist control as it was during Batista's early regime. Six of us refused to sign the pact, but then four relented under pressure, leaving one other delegate and myself. We were both stripped of our rank and turned over to a Communist battalion as prisoners.

"However, Ché Guevara could not risk a scandal in the labor movement at that point, so our court martial was postponed. After January 1, I was set free because of the intercession of David Salvador, who was then the head of the Labor Section of the 26th of July Movement."

Rodríguez Quesada then became secretary general of

the CTC in Las Villas province, and was elected to the executive board of the National Federation of Sugar Workers. Thus he was in the front lines of the battle for the control of Cuban labor, which reached a climax late in 1959. Vicente Rubiera Feíto, another veteran anti-Communist labor leader, was less fortunate. His expulsion from the CTC, and the Communist capture of the National Federation of Telephone Workers which he headed, took place within the first sixty days of the Castro regime, and should have revealed (but unfortunately did not) the exact shape of things to come.

Rubiera had been president of the 1947 Congress of the CTC which purged the Cuban labor movement of the Communist hierarchy, headed by Lázaro Peña, installed originally in 1940 as a result of the party's deal with Fulgencio Batista. Thus, Vicente Rubiera was a marked man; but there were even more urgent reasons for the Communists' early assault on the telephone union.

"The telephone workers," says Rubiera, "unlike many other unions, were an integral part of the revolution, which makes it seem even more strange that we should be the first to be destroyed. The best evidence of our loyalty was the smoothness with which the telephone system worked during the critical hours after Batista's downfall. Off-duty operators and maintenance personnel reported immediately and voluntarily for extra duty. During the general strike they slept in the exchanges and even went without food in some cases, but the extra-heavy traffic was handled efficiently.

"However, the Communist take-over began on January 1 while we were still working in the guarded telephone building. We had only a few Communists in the Havana local, but they immediately assumed authority. The local leaders were thrust aside, and I was informed that I had been deposed as chief officer of the national federation. This was impossible, of course, under our by-laws, but apparently the by-laws no longer applied. These usurpers showed us as their authority a directive signed by the seven-member 'revolutionary committee' placed in control of the CTC by Ché Guevara.

"On February 13 an assembly of the National Federation of Telephone Workers was convened in the CTC headquarters in Havana to settle the matter of union leadership. This we welcomed because we knew that in our strongly anti-Communist federation we had more than enough votes to win. However, when we arrived at the auditorium, which seats about 2,000, we found it jammed with people who were not even telephone workers. The front rows were occupied entirely by strangers and we had to find seats in the rear.

"The group on the platform, I noticed, was much more distinguished than at our usual meetings. For example, there were three cabinet members, and the principal speaker was Camilo Cienfuegos, chief of staff of the Revolutionary Army and one of the great heroes of the revolution. They were there to give the proceedings the authority of the regime.

"When the meeting got under way the chairman resorted to the old Communist trick of refusing to recognize delegates who were in opposition. Twice I tried to get the floor and was ignored. Then, when I attempted to speak anyway, the armed militiamen, obviously under orders, leveled their machine guns at me. A total stranger came to us and warned that we would be shot if we persisted in disrupting the meeting. Finally, we were forced to leave.

"After our departure the Communist-approved slate of officers was elected by voice vote. The anti-Communist leaders, including myself, were deprived of all privileges including our right to vote on union matters. Then we were formally expelled from the federation.

"The reason behind all this became clear on March 4

when the government 'intervened' in the Cuban Telephone Company, which was the first step toward outright confiscation. Within the three weeks since our expulsion, of course, the Communists had established complete control over the company's management and operating personnel."

# Part Two

# TEMPLE OR TOMB?

Humberto Medrano, former assistant editor of *Prensa Libre,* Havana's largest daily newspaper, remembers lying in a barber's chair on the morning of January 10, 1959, eyes closed, face lathered, listening to the excited, high-pitched voices throughout the huge shop.

"Fidel Castro had made his triumphant entrance into Havana two days before," he says. "Nearly forty-eight hours later everybody was still talking joyously and confidently about the inspiring speech he had made at Camp Columbia. Listening to this *potpourri* of praise, the thought occurred to me, 'This is the voice of Cuba. And everyone is passionately for Fidel!'

"Surely this unanimous praise must sound like celestial music to Castro's ears. Yet, at the same time, he must feel some anxiety, some grave concern for the tasks that lie ahead. For one cannot arouse in a people such passionate faith and devotion without feeling a tremendous sense of responsibility to justify that faith by fulfilling the people's hopes and aspirations.

"I began to think of an editorial for the next day's paper. The title would be 'A Tiger by the Tail.' Even as I was being shaved, with the barber talking incessantly, the article wrote itself in my mind. Until now, I said, Fidel Castro has waged war, and war is destruction. From now on it will be necessary for him to govern, and governing means building. To destroy is easy; one need only light a fuse or strike a percussion cap to blow up a bridge. But to build a bridge requires capacity, patience, discipline, and a sense of responsibility. Let Commandante Castro not forget that many moral and legal bridges have been blown up during the Batista tyranny. These bridges must be rebuilt. The first great bridge which must be restored is the Constitution of 1940, because we must traverse that bridge to find a decent, peaceful and honorable national life.

"That was the substance of the piece I wrote that day. There was nothing prophetic or important about it, except the quotation I happened to think of as a closing paragraph. The words were those of Louis Antoine de Saint-Just, the 'Archangel of the French Revolution,' who said, 'The stones are cut for the building of freedom. You can build either a temple or a tomb with the same stones.'

"For some reason, which I didn't understand at the time, Fidel Castro was offended by that editorial. So were many of our readers. The vast majority of Cubans were convinced that Fidel Castro was building the temple of freedom. Even to imply anything to the contrary was heresy. Fidel was then a god who, in time, would make everything right!

"During the spring of 1959, Fidel Castro had the people mesmerized. He was on the radio and television constantly, and he talked on and on for hours at a time. The people listened and believed every word he said. They put stickers on the windshields of their cars saying 'Thank you, Fidel!' Signs appeared on the doors and windows of houses: 'Fidel, my house is yours!'

"Castro denied, repeatedly and angrily, that there were Communists in the government. The revolution, he declared, was 'not red but olive-green.' He promised that there would be no more dictatorship, no more bloodshed. Free elections would be held, he said, 'within eighteen months—more or less.' Political parties would be permitted to organize 'within eight or ten months.' It sounded wonderful.

"A few brave souls dared to inquire why he already had allowed the Communists to organize as Cuba's only legal party. 'The constitution has been restored,' Fidel replied testily. 'We don't want to take away any of the liberties Cubans had before Batista scrapped the constitution. There is no reason to be afraid of the Communists, as long as they obey the laws.'

"This, of course, was evasive and inconsistent. But few Cubans took particular notice or, if they did, they remained silent. Even those who found things to criticize directed their criticism against the regime and carefully refrained from placing any of the blame on Fidel Castro, who was beyond reproach."

### *Revolutionary Justice*

Still, there were some Cubans who were in a position to see the idol's feet of clay. Father Jorge Bez Chabebe, chaplain of the Catholic Youth Movement in Santiago de Cuba, was attending a banquet on Saturday, January 10, honoring the U.S. Vice Consul, when another priest, Father Rafael Escala, approached the table and whispered: "Please come with me, Father. Four Batista officers are to be tried and executed tonight. We will be needed."

Says Father Jorge: "The finality of the words 'tried *and* executed' made me shudder. How could one know, even before the trial, that the verdict would be guilty and the sentence death? However, I said nothing but went with Father Escala. That was the beginning of many horrible experiences."

The two priests went to the municipal court and found it crowded with the families of prisoners who might or might not be tried that night. The "judges" on the bench were five rebel army men only one of whom, according to Father Jorge, had any knowledge of law.

"Charges were read, prosecution witnesses testified briefly," the priest recalls. "The judges dozed, or conversed among themselves, paying no attention to the proceedings. At one point, Raúl Castro came in and chatted with the judges. Thus, the 'trials' dragged on from ten o'clock that night until two o'clock the next morning. Then the list of names was read and the death sentence pronounced for all.

"Father Escala and I went out into a courtyard and climbed into an army truck. There were fourteen prisoners already in the truck, only four of whom I had seen in court. The others apparently had been condemned without trial."

On the way to the Campo de Tiro (rifle range) in the San Juan hills the two priests heard confessions, administered last rites, and even baptized one man. Those who are about to die usually face the confessor with naked souls. More than once Father Jorge had the sickening awareness that an innocent man was about to die.

"There were several other trucks at the rifle range when we arrived," says Father Jorge, "making the number of men to be executed about fifty-five or sixty. There were also two other priests. For the next six hours we heard confessions as the men went before the firing squad, usually two at a time. The bodies were allowed to fall into a deep trench. It was nearly ten o'clock in the morning when the last volley was fired. The last thing I saw, as the truck started back to Santiago, was a heavy bulldozer pushing the mounds of earth into the common grave.

"I remembered what Fidel Castro had said only a few days earlier: 'I promise to solve every problem without bloodshed. I promise Cuban mothers that no more shots will be fired.' Yet I couldn't get the awful sounds of rifle fire and the sickening thud of dead bodies from my mind. I kept wondering, 'What is happening to Cuba?'"

Cuban lawyers were among the first to recognize the frightening developments that were taking place behind the false front of Castro's "revolutionary justice." Dr. Domingo Acosta, a Havana lawyer, spent his days and nights in La Cabaña Fortress where three or four military courts, convened in officers' clubs and movie theaters, worked around the clock to feed the firing squads. "Some of my clients were in the death cells," Dr. Acosta says, "even before their cases came before the courts. There were no written charges or verdicts; the only records were the death lists to which names were added. In many instances I found these lists 'signed' with the thumbprints of illiterate judges. Appeals were denied by rubber stamp and without hearings. Defense lawyers were despised and browbeaten. I saw cases where a five- or ten-year sentence was doubled arbitrarily merely because the verdict was appealed."

Dr. Francisco Cosío, another lawyer, says: "Bank accounts were seized and property was confiscated on the flimsy charge that the owner was a *Batistiano*. In many cases the victim was a plain civil servant who had been in the government for years and was innocent of any wrongdoing. There were many cases in which people lost property and the savings of a lifetime merely because they had the same common Cuban name as someone who worked for Batista. But to a lawyer the greatest horror was that there was no legal recourse against such injustices."

"Castro told the people that the Constitution of 1940 was in force," says Dr. Emilio Maza y Rodríguez, Havana law professor. "But the constitution prohibited the death penalty. The constitution specified that 'no one shall be tried or condemned other than by a competent judge or court, and by virtue of laws in existence prior to the crime.' Nevertheless, during the first fortnight of the Castro regime more than 500 persons were condemned to death by *incompetent* courts which illegally applied penal laws which were drawn up in the Sierra Maestra in 1958."

On February 7, 1959, the Constitution of 1940 was straitjacketed in a new "Fundamental Law" which sanctioned the death penalty and confiscation of property—even for *political* crimes—and permitted the *retroactive* application of penal laws. It also vested all power in the Council of Ministers, thus opening the way for further abuses. Says Dr. Maza: "For all practical purposes, the rule of law in Cuba was already dead."

The Council of Ministers, exercising its new power to amend Cuban law at will, on February 10, 1959, lowered the required age for the presidency and premiership from 35 years to 30. Three days later, Dr. José Miró Cardona resigned and Fidel Castro became Prime Minister.

"At that moment," says Father Jorge, "a most unusual trial was going on in Santiago de Cuba. The prisoners were forty-three pilots, gunners and crewmen who had served in Batista's air force. They were charged with 'genocide' for having bombed cities and villages in Oriente province during the civil war. The prosecutor, at Fidel Castro's orders, demanded the death penalty.

"However, this court was a good one. The presiding officer was Major Félix Pena, a commander of the rebel army, whom I knew and respected. There was only the flimsiest sort of evidence to support the charges that these particular fliers had been responsible for civilian deaths, so the court acquitted the forty-three fliers.

"In Havana, Fidel Castro heard the news and flew into a rage. He ordered the verdict set aside, removed Félix Pena from the court, and sent Augusto Martínez Sánchez, his Minister of Defense, to Santiago to conduct a new trial. This was what Cuba's hard-pressed jurists had been waiting for. The national and provincial bar associations vigorously protested this flagrant violation of the legal principle which protects the accused from being placed in double jeopardy. Coming from Castro, who was himself a lawyer, this was an unpardonable breach of law.

"But Castro was adamant, and he again demanded the death penalty. So the second trial was held. This time the defense counsel for the fliers was the distinguished lawyer, Dr. Carlos Peña Jústiz, who had defended Fidel Castro in the Moncada Barracks case. 'If you condemn these men,' Peña Jústiz warned the court, 'you will succeed only in making Fidel Castro the new Napoleon of the Caribbean.' Martínez Sánchez denounced this remark as 'infamous, ill-intentioned, and counter-revolutionary.' The court refused to apply the death penalty, but sentenced the men to prison terms ranging from twenty to thirty years.

"Major Félix Pena, who was widely respected, was quietly summoned to Havana by President Urrutia and told that he was to be sent abroad as a military attaché. Two days later, Pena was found slumped in the front seat of his car at Camp Columbia with a bullet through his heart. The official verdict was suicide, but the circumstances looked very suspicious.

"Dr. Carlos Peña Jústiz remained at liberty but lived under a cloud. Later he was imprisoned as a counter-revolutionary and there is doubt whether he is still alive. The case of the Batista fliers left deep scars, and gave Fidel something to worry about."

Angry, arrogant Fidel Castro declared: "We shall be respectful of the law, but of the revolutionary law. For the old law, no respect! For the new law, respect! Who has the right to modify the constitution? The majority! Who has the majority? The revolution!"

### *"Fidel is Worried"*

Dr. Luis Benítez picked up his newspaper on the morning of March 7 and read that Fidel Castro's Cabinet had passed a decree ordering reductions in residential rents ranging up to fifty per cent. "Since I owned no property and rented my home," he says, "this was basically good news. According to the decree, my rent would be cut thirty per cent. But, then, I began to wonder. What would this do to property values? At this rate, who would undertake to build the new housing which Cuba needed badly?

"Several days later, one of my patients, who was a deputy minister in the government, came to see me and I asked him about the new rent law. 'We simply had to do something,' he said. 'Since these trials Fidel's popularity has gone down at least ten points.' I laughed and asked him if we were now being governed by public opinion polls.

" 'You don't understand,' he said. 'The revolution is not yet consolidated. Fidel is worried. He has only a few men he can really trust aside from Ché and Raúl. Until things are under control we must proceed very cautiously.'

"Then he looked at me sharply, and stopped talking. He never came to see me again. This fellow was not a Communist, although he was something of a leftist. But he worshiped Fidel Castro and would have followed him blindly into anything. So far as I know, he is still in the Castro regime."

Fidel Castro announced that he was coming to Santiago, and Gerardo Abascal made plans to meet him. "This time I was not alone," says Abascal. "By now, many of my old friends in the 26th of July group shared my misgivings. The Communists controlled virtually everything in Santiago—the newspapers and the municipal and provincial governments. Their leader was Major Manuel Piñeiro, a redheaded beast who was called *Barba Roja* [Red Beard]. Piñeiro also had a deputy named Major Calixto García, also a Communist, who later succeeded him as commander of the military district.

"We made an appointment to meet Fidel, and it was

agreed that I should act as spokesman for the delegation. When we arrived at the faculty hall of the university, where the meeting was to take place, Piñeiro, García and the other Communists we intended to complain about were present at the meeting with Fidel. My colleagues decided that, under the circumstances, it would be unwise for me to speak as planned. However, I was determined to go ahead with it.

"I told Fidel that we came to him as old friends and loyal supporters of the revolution. 'We are distressed by the way things are going in Oriente,' I said. 'The administration is lax, the promised reforms are not being made, yet we are powerless to do anything about it. As members of the 26th of July Movement, we are ready to make any sacrifice, willing to perform any duties. But since we are not Communists our services are not wanted by this administration. We are always kept on the outside.'

"Piñeiro and the others were staring at me coldly. But I went on and told Castro that we believed that the 26th of July Revolution had to succeed in Oriente, the 'cradle of the revolution,' as well as in Santiago, which he had called the future capital of Cuba. 'We must lead the way,' I said, 'and set the example for Cuba. We are convinced that the revolution can succeed according to the principles which you, Fidel, proclaimed from the Sierra Maestra, and without borrowing from the ideology of Soviet or Chinese Communism.'

"Fidel Castro, of course, is a master at handling such situations. He showed no sign of anger or embarrassment. He just talked! He talked about his plans, about the future of Cuba, about his devotion to Oriente province. But he never once mentioned communism, or the Communist control of our press and government, or even the utter helplessness of the 26th of July Movement. When he finished talking, the meeting was over. He left the room with his Communist entourage. We were right back where we started."

Shortly after the Abascal confrontation, however, José Manuel Berenguer, co-owner of Santiago Station CMKC and the Oriente radio network, was summoned to Havana by Castro.

"Fidel was angry, hurt, even plaintive," says Berenguer. "He accused us of 'growing cold' toward the revolution. He said he was amazed to find Santiago, of all places, full of 'counter-revolutionaries.' He wanted to know what had gone wrong, what we could do to win back the loyalty of these people.

"I explained that many of his old friends in Oriente province were disappointed because he had done nothing to redeem his promise to make Santiago the capital or even a federal district. I also told him that there was growing concern over the way the Communists were taking charge of everything. At the mention of communism Fidel flared up.

"He said he was tired of hearing all this talk about communism. 'This is a socialist revolution,' he declared. 'We are pledged to make socialist reforms for the good of our people. What do you expect us to do—turn Cuba over to the international bankers and imperialists?' "

" 'What do you mean by socialism, Fidel?' I asked. 'Do you mean the welfare state, like the socialism of British labor? Do you mean the kind of socialism they have in Sweden? Or are you talking about Soviet socialism—communism?'

" 'I'm talking about *Cuban* socialism!' he shouted. 'People's socialism—our own brand of national socialism!' Then he added, vaguely, 'Maybe something nearer to what Tito has done in Yugoslavia.'

"After that, he changed the subject. He became more conciliatory, and began to talk about how much we could help in restoring people's faith in the revolution. He revived his plan to help us build up our Oriente stations and start another national network. Enrique Oltuski, the Minister of Communications, was called in, and he said that BANFAIC [the government development bank] would lend us $200,000 to get started. But when we left the meeting, my partner shook his head sadly. 'José,' he said, 'this is hopeless. We have been fighting for a lost cause.'

"But on the way back to Santiago we decided that we couldn't give up," says Berenguer. "We made plans to increase our broadcasts exposing Communist infiltration. We started a 'regional' campaign, based on the theme that the people of Oriente province, who had fought and won the revolution, had a sacred responsibility to save the revolution from the Communist perversion. But we carefully avoided any attacks on Fidel personally. The people wouldn't stand for that—they were still for him. Even my own family would not believe me when I told them what Fidel had confessed to us in Havana.

"Soon after these broadcasts started, Major Calixto García paid us a visit. He told us that Fidel was very angry because we had joined the counter-revolutionaries. He said that our broadcasts were 'destroying national unity.' García warned us that if the broadcasts did not cease or change, we would be out of business.

"Of course, we heard no more from Oltuski about the government loan. Then we began to lose the good people on our staff; the unions replaced them with announcers and engineers who were either Communists or Communist sympathizers. After that, we knew, it was only a matter of time."

### *Seeds of Doubt*

During the spring of 1959, Alonso León, sales supervisor of the soap company, traveled regularly through Cuba with a sharp ear tuned to public opinion. "Despite everything," he says, "Fidel's popularity was still high. Occasionally, you would hear doubts or criticism. But such opinions were seldom voiced openly; you heard them privately and confidentially from people who knew you well."

One day in early May, Alonso León, accompanied by a district manager, stopped to have a drink in a small café somewhere in Camagüey. There were only a few customers in the place, but León began to speak in a loud voice, extolling Fidel Castro for the speech he had made on television the night before. As he spoke he became aware of a tall, barrel-chested man, dressed in rough work clothes, who was glaring at him contemptuously. Soon the stranger spoke, not to León, but to his companion.

"Your friend," he said, pointing to León, "reminds me of Fidel. He talks, talks, talks, but never stops to use his head!"

"We laughed," Alonso recalls, "and I said that many of my best friends told me that I talked too much. Then we shook hands and I invited the fellow to have a drink. He told us that he had a small business, with four or five trucks, delivering charcoal and sometimes kerosene and fuel oil."

"You know," the fuel dealer said, "not long ago I was just like you—a real *Fidelista.* I would sit in front of my television listening to him by the hour and saying, 'Oh, Fidel, you are a genius, a smart man, a great leader! How can anyone know so much about so many things?'

"But then one night, as I was listening, Fidel began to talk about Cuba's fuel problems and what he was going to do about them. Suddenly I sat up and said, 'No, no, Fidel! That is not correct. Someone has given you the wrong information!' But Fidel went right on talking nonsense.

"This made me think. 'Here, for the first time,' I told

myself, 'Fidel talks about something I *really* know—fuel, charcoal, oil, kerosene—and he is all wrong. I have been in this business all my life, and my father before me. So I *know* that what Fidel says is nonsense!' So, I wondered, how about when he talks of things that I *don't* know?

"I decided to find out. I bought a long wire and put my television on the front porch. I got a tub and filled it with ice and lots of beer, *malta* and Coca Cola. When Fidel was to speak I invited many neighbors to come and have a drink and listen with me.

"Now when Fidel talked about raising more cattle per acre, I would say, 'Hey, Miguel, you work with cows—what is this he says?' If he talked about the things he planned to do with sugar, I would say, 'José, you grind the cane. Can you do what Fidel says?' I did the same thing whether he spoke of tomatoes or housing or building roads—there was always someone there who knew.

"Each time I would see the puzzled, worried look on their faces. No one liked to say that Fidel was wrong. But there it was! When we talked things over, compared notes, we all began to wonder: How could Fidel talk so much and be wrong about so many thing? Pretty soon the neighbors stopped coming. But that was all right with me. I didn't listen to Fidel much myself any more."

Says Alonso León: "Our friend, the charcoal dealer, sat sipping his beer in silence for a moment. Here, I thought, is a simple, intelligent man who has seen a frightening thing in the hero he worshiped. How many more average Cubans are there, I wondered, who are like him and his neighbors?

"Just then he got up from the table, put on his weathered straw sombrero, and held out his hand.

" 'You know what I think, *amigo?*' he asked, with a sad smile. 'I think Fidel Castro is *fooling* the people!' "

### *The Promised Land*

During the early days of the regime, Fidel Castro on numerous occasions reiterated his promise to "turn all tenant farmers into landowners." He did nothing to discourage reports, widely circulated, that the forthcoming "agrarian reform law" was one drafted in the Sierra Maestra by Humberto Sorí Marín, judge advocate of the rebel army, who had become the first Minister of Agriculture in the revolutionary government. Sorí Marín's law, according to these reports, implemented the provisions in the Constitution of 1940 and would distribute to landless peasants extensive state-owned lands as well as the idle or uncultivated land under private ownership. "Nothing is more certain," Castro declared, "than our giving land to the *campesinos*. The reform will comprise all of the Sierra Maestra law, and furthermore will make landlords give land to those who have none. There must not be a *campesino* left who is without land."

While there was a strong note of demagoguery in Castro's statements, few Cuban landowners, large or small, showed any apprehension or panic over the coming reforms. "The reason for this," says Carlos Rafael Menció, a lawyer and small landowner (33 acres), "was that in Cuba we had a very legalistic concept of private property and ownership. There was a 'rule of right' which assured the owner of fair compensation for any private property confiscated by the state. So the large landowners, even if they disagreed with the objectives of the law and were reluctant to part with any land, knew or expected that they would be fairly compensated."

One large landowner (100,000 acres) adds: "There was another reason. Agrarian reform, in terms of 'making every landless peasant a landowner,' had always been an impractical scheme and a political football. Everyone in rural Cuba, whether he was a landowner or a tenant, knew this. To give the average peasant a tract of land and nothing else would be cruel punishment. What he needed was tools, machinery, fertilizers, insecticides and, above all, know-how. But even this represented only one phase of the problem. The kind of 'agrarian reform' Cuba needed, and what we all were hoping for, was really 'agricultural development'—crop diversification, cultivation, irrigation, insect controls, and above all more and better rural roads, highways, schools, sanitation and health facilities.

"Why did idle or uncultivated lands exist in Cuba, both under state and private ownership? Because these lands were located in isolated regions, far from roads and highways which could bring any possible production to markets, mills, storage plants, factories. To settle small farmers on such lands without proper access to towns, markets, schools, health centers, and so forth, obviously would be a cruel folly."

### *The Gains That Were Lost*

The Cuban consensus in early 1959 is well expressed by Dr. Menció. "The demagogic or politician's approach to agrarian reform," he says, "obscured or overlooked certain facts which made the problems of rural Cuba totally unlike those anywhere else in the Americas. Before 1959 the old 'sugar monoculture' had ceased to be the monster which had a stranglehold on the Cuban economy. The sugar coordination laws had set a series of quotas which legally reduced cane cultivation to sound economic levels. The same legislation guaranteed an equitable distribution of profits to all concerned in sugar production—landowners, colonists, tenant farmers, sugar workers, with the workers getting the greatest profits of all time. Equally important, these laws made land available for the production of other products—coffee, cacao, tobacco, fruits, vegetables, and livestock.

"The demagogic approach also, unfortunately, pictured the Cuban peasant and tenant farmer as an impoverished, depressed being who lived at the mercy of the cruel landowner. This was a fantastic distortion of the truth, as every inhabitant of rural Cuba was aware. As long ago as 1937, laws were passed in Cuba which gave the colonist or tenant who raised sugar cane a 'security of tenure.' Under this law the owner forfeited all right to the land except to a rent which was fixed by the Sugar Coordination Act. The tenant could not be dispossessed so long as he produced and paid rent. The right of tenure could be inherited, sold or mortgaged. If a new owner purchased the land he had to assume these obligations contracted by the previous owner.

"Between 1948 and 1952 this 'security of tenure' was extended to all tenants, sub-tenant and even squatters on Cuban farmlands. The only condition was that rent must be paid, and the rental rates were fixed, not by the landowner, but by the legislative decrees. So, for all practical purposes, before 1959 the tenant farmers of Cuba were their own masters."

[This generally unknown aspect of the land laws of pre-Castro Cuba was emphasized in the report of the International Commission of Jurists, *Cuba and the Rule of Law,* published in Geneva in November 1962. "At the time Fidel Castro took power," the report stated, "all the tenant farmers in Cuba were already assured of a security of tenure of their land, for which they paid very low rents. . . . The Cuban tenant farmer had many of the rights which are normally associated with full ownership of land but without the obligations which are usually involved. Conversely, the Cuban system did not encourage the tenant farmer to make long-term plans to expand output and improve the soil."]

Humberto Medrano, who was neither landowner nor farmer, but a journalist who had made a careful study of Cuba's agrarian problems, interjects this comment: "We cannot say truthfully that rural Cuba was a *Jauja* [Utopia]. It is undeniable that enormous tracts of land still remained in the hands of a few wealthy owners. It is undeniable also that part, but only a relatively small part, of the rural population lacked arable land, proper tools and equipment, modern agricultural training, adequate health, medical and educational facilities. But it is equally undeniable that the majority of people in rural Cuba—landowners, tenants, members of the free cooperatives—were working the land conscientiously, profitably and happily and were making great progress.

"The Constitution of 1940, which even outlawed the *latifundium* [large landholdings], provided all the juridical powers necessary for constructive and legal agrarian reforms. What Cuba needed was a government which would carry out the constitutional mandate honestly and courageously, within the juridical and legal framework, and without granting immoral concessions or indulging in demagogic excesses."

Señor Evelio Mederos, landowner (1,000 acres), commercial farmer, and former president of the Cuban Association of Fruit and Vegetable Exporters, adds this observation: "Everyone thought, when agrarian reform was discussed early in 1959, that the first consideration would be the industrialization of agricultural production, transportation, storage, markets, etc. Cuba could produce even greater quantities of vegetables, both for domestic consumption and for export, during the months from September to May when the rainy season begins. But we lacked sufficient means to store, preserve and process them. In short, Cuba had an agricultural capacity fully trained and prepared to increase production of the usual crops and to embark upon the cultivation of new crops.

That is where the government might have helped with realistic agrarian development or reform. Everyone in Cuba would have benefited."

### *The Law of Everything—and Nothing*

The long-awaited Agrarian Reform Law was signed on May 17, 1959, at a ceremonial meeting held (for publicity purposes) in a little village high in the Sierra Maestra. Castro, President Urrutia and most cabinet ministers were present. However, Minister of Agriculture Humberto Sorí Marín was conspicuously absent. Close associates say that he was shocked by the law he saw in the final draft, and refused to sign it—although his name was appended arbitrarily to the law itself. Even from the bare outline published in the press (the full text was not made available until June) many Cubans also realized that the "reforms" went far beyond the provisions of Sierra Maestra Law No. 3 and the spirit of the 1940 Constitution.

The Agrarian Reform Law of 1959 limited the holdings of any individual, family or corporation to 990 acres, unless the land was devoted to sugar cane, rice or cattle-raising, in which case the maximum holding was set at 3,300 acres. Foreigners were denied the right to own or acquire Cuban land, and land could be held by a corporation only if all stockholders were Cuban citizens. Excess land expropriated would be paid for in 20-year government bonds bearing 4½ per cent interest, but the purchase price would be based on the assessed value rather than the real value of the property.

Every *campesino* was to get a "vital minimum" of 66 acres, which appeared to redeem Fidel's promise of "land for the landless." Not until later, however, did the *campesinos* learn that the "vital minimum" could not be sold or mortgaged, or even be bequeathed to more than one member of the family. But there was an even more subtle catch: the land so distributed had to be developed "by agrarian cooperatives whenever possible."

On June 12, a few days before the full text of the law was published, Humberto Sorí Marín resigned as Minister of Agriculture.* With him went four other "moderates" in the Cabinet—Foreign Minister Roberto Agramonte, Interior Minister Luis Orlando Rodríguez, Health Minister Julio Martínez Pérez, and Welfare Minister Elena Mederos. The five posts were filled by Communists or dependable leftists.

What had happened? There are several versions which differ only in small details. "Behind Sorí Marín's back," says Señor Alberto Fernández, who at the time was head of Castro's Sugar Stabilization Institute, "Fidel Castro had allowed his Communist colleagues to transform Sorí Marín's Sierra Maestra Law No. 3 into a radical reform which was designed to serve specifically as the cornerstone of Cuba's Communist economy."

Dr. Jorge Castellanos offers the details: "Sometime in the spring of 1958, Dr. Delfin Rodríguez, a physician who was with Fidel in the Sierra Maestra, took the draft of Sorí Marín's law to the Communist leader, Rafael Rodríguez [no relation], who was then living at Boca Ciega, a beach near Havana. Rafael Rodríguez scrapped Sorí Marín's law as too bourgeois, and wrote a new law which he took with him to the Sierra when he joined forces with Fidel in September. Some months later, two other Communists, Antonio Núñez Jiménez and Oscar Pino Santos, helped Carlos Rafael put the finishing touches to the draft which became the Agrarian Reform Law of 1959. During all this time, Sorí Marín was kept in the dark as to what was going on.

* Humberto Sorí Marín subsequently became active in the anti-Castro underground, was captured at the ill-fated "unity" meeting of March 18, and was executed by firing squad in La Cabaña on April 20, 1961. (See pages 102 and 121.)

"The steel trap in this law was Chapter VII, which created the National Agrarian Reform Institute (INRA) as 'an autonomous entity with its own juridical personality.' INRA was to become the super-state, actually the Communist apparatus which set the stage for taking over agriculture, commerce, industry, the entire economy. Naturally, the president of INRA was Fidel Castro. But it is significant that, from the start, the top jobs were given to proved Communists. Antonio Núñez Jiménez became executive director, Oscar Pino Santos was in charge of production. Ché Guevara became head of the all-important industry section; he also imported a lot of trained Communists from Chile to serve as administrators. Later, on February 13, 1962, Fidel Castro stepped down and Rafael Rodríguez was rewarded by being made president of INRA, the Communist super-state he had created."

### *Between the Lines*

Strangely, it was not the foreigners or the large landowners who registered the first protests against the new law. "They and their lawyers were too busy studying the law and looking for loopholes," says Ernesto Santamarina, whose family owned a farm and cattle ranch in Camagüey. "The small and medium-size farmers and ranchers were the first to feel the squeeze. And we made a painful discovery. The lawyers were wasting their time, because the Agrarian Reform Law didn't mean a thing—not even what it said. The local bureaucrats of INRA were free to interpret the law to suit themselves!"

The old and large Santamarina family owned nearly 5,000 acres of land, which was about 1,700 acres more than the maximum the law allowed. "But all this was highly developed land," says Señor Santamarina, "devoted to the production of sugar cane, cattle as well as vegetables and fruits. We had about 300 acres of the finest citrus groves in Cuba. We had put in our own irrigation system, our own wells, our own power plant, even our own roads. We made money and so did the thirty-three tenants who operated the farms and ranches. Farmers and ranchers used to come from all over Cuba to study our advanced methods of irrigation, fumigation, crop diversification, and cattle breeding.

"Under the stated terms of the law, we expected to keep 3,300 acres. But early in June we got the bad news. The local INRA chief, a former rebel army officer, ruled that under the law we were entitled to only 990 acres. I knew what the law said, and I put up a stiff argument. But I got nowhere. INRA, I discovered, was a 'juridical entity,' a law unto itself, and its decisions could not be appealed to the conventional courts of law.

"Dividing up the land, taking part of the fruit orchards, part of the grazing lands, part of the cane fields threatened to wreck the whole operation, both for us and for the state as well. But that wasn't the worst of it. The INRA chief ruled that since we had 600 head of cattle on the original pasture land, we were entitled to keep only 180 head on the land left to us. I went to him with a copy of the law in my hand. 'Show me where this law gives you any authority to confiscate cattle,' I demanded. He laughed at me and threw the law into his wastebasket.

" 'That law means nothing,' he said. 'It was obsolete before it was published. Orders are the only thing that count here, and we have been ordered to take cattle.'

"They came and took away 345 head of our cattle, without paying a single peso. I never even got a receipt. But I soon found out that the same thing was happening all over the province. The prize herds, which had helped Cuba build up a great new industry, producing more meat per capita than any country in the hemisphere, were being ruined. The fools were even slaughtering the prize breeding animals and shipping the frozen meat to Russia."

Early in June thousands of small tobacco farmers in Pinar del Río province organized mass meetings to protest against the arbitrary—and illegal—land seizures which they said were ruining an important national industry.

"These INRA officials," said a spokesman, "are taking land away from the small tobacco farmers in the name of the national interest, when in reality they are deliberately wrecking the foundations of our national economy."

Said one small farmer: "I am not afraid of being called a counter-revolutionist because I defend what belongs to me. I will continue to defend my land as long as I can breathe. What they want to take away from me is mine. I obtained it by great sacrifice and with the sweat of my brow, and it is all I have to leave my children."

Fidel Castro heard these pleas and protests and reacted angrily. "We will not change even a comma in the Agrarian Reform Law," he declared. "The agrarian reform program will move forward, even if it rains railway spikes!"

### *Commissars of the New Order*

Few Cubans knew or even suspected what went on in the imposing but unfinished twenty-story building facing on the Plaza Cívica in midtown Havana. They knew that, in the last days of the Batista regime, it had been erected as the new city hall but had never been occupied by the municipal administration. They were aware that now, in the spring of 1959, it was the headquarters of INRA, the administrative agency of Agrarian Reform. But that was all they knew. The armed guards allowed no one to enter the building without a pass, and special passes were needed to gain access to specific upper floors. With a few exceptions, no one but Communists and trusted leftists knew exactly what went on behind the closed and guarded doors.

One exception, however, was Dr. Manuel F. Artime, a devout Roman Catholic and a staunch anti-Communist. In the spring of 1959, Dr. Artime was probably the first and last of his kind to be passed through the guarded portals of the INRA skyscraper and allowed to listen to the unguarded deliberations of the new commissars. It was a hair-raising experience.

Dr. Artime, physician and educator, had been part of an independent anti-Batista movement in the province of Pinar del Río when, late in 1958, he agreed to go into the Sierra Maestra and join the rebel army. The purpose, as explained to him by Father Armando Llorente and other anti-Batista Catholics, was to counteract the Communist infiltration of the revolutionary forces.

However, the revolution ended even before Dr. Artime could get his work started. But he was so shocked by the strength of the Communists among the peasants as well as in the rebel army that he decided to stay on in Oriente province as an agent of the agrarian bureau of Humberto Sorí Marín's new Ministry of Agriculture. His subsequent performance in organizing farm and fishery cooperatives was so impressive that, when the Agrarian Reform Law was enacted in May, he was appointed deputy chief of INRA Zone 0-22 in Oriente province.

"Commander René Vallejo, the chief of Zone 0-22," says Dr. Artime, "had promised to take me to one of the confidential meetings of INRA which were held in Havana each month. He kept his word, and one day in June we flew to Havana in his military plane, and the next morning we presented our credentials to the guards in the headquarters building on the Plaza Cívica and were admitted to a conference chamber on one of the upper floors.

"Ché Guevara, Pino Santos, Waldo Medina, Antonio Núñez Jiménez, director of INRA, and others were present, but Castro had not yet arrived. The others were the chiefs of the twenty-six INRA zones, accompanied by deputies and assistants like myself.

"Núñez Jiménez opened the meeting by warning us that these meetings were confidential: 'Nothing said or discussed here must pass beyond the walls of this room. We are concerned here with the true objectives of the revolution, and these involve many things which the people are not yet ready to assimilate.'

"Then he said something that I had suspected for some time; nevertheless the bold statement shocked me. 'You understand that, as delegates of INRA, you represent the real government of Cuba. INRA is the true Cuban state; all other government institutions are pure sham.' INRA chiefs were omnipotent in their zones, he said; they had behind them all the powers of the police, army, navy, judiciary, even the Council of Ministers and the President himself. They were, in other words, the commissars of the New Order!

"Fidel Castro made his entrance," Artime recalls, "and we stood up and saluted while he took the presidential chair. He began by stating that INRA was spending enormous amounts of money and making some great economic blunders. He mentioned the development in the Zapata Swamp as a horrible example.

" 'However, let's not worry about money,' he laughed. 'When the treasury is empty, we can always confiscate the money in the banks! Why not? When the state has absolute control of the economy that will be simple. Let us see who dares to oppose us when we are confronted with a hungry population! This is something that Karl Marx never dreamed of,' he said proudly. 'Hunger will be the midwife attending the birth of a socialist state in Cuba.'

"Castro boasted that soon Cuban investors would have to be 'geniuses' in order to find places to put their money. 'If you doubt this,' he said, 'stop and think for a moment.

Where will they invest? In houses? We already have the rent law, and there is something even more drastic in preparation. In land? With INRA in operation they would be crazy to invest in land! In industry? Only over Ché's dead body! So the investors will have to eat their money, or keep it in the banks—where Ché can get it!' "

Artime listened, dumbfounded. If someone had told him these things he would not have believed them; yet now he heard them from Fidel's own lips.

"Pino Santos brought up the fact that no land was actually being given to the people as had been promised, and that the *guajiros* [peasants] were getting restless. This time it was Núñez Jiménez who gave the totally cynical answer: 'We will do nothing about that, except in a few cases where the *guajiros* become too insistent. Then we will divide up a little land, take photographs of the presentation, make much publicity. That ought to keep them quiet for a time!'

"The question arose as to how and when owners of confiscated land were to be indemnified. Fidel waved his cigar and replied airily: 'They will be paid with bonds, eventually, and at our price, not theirs!' Ché Guevara laughed and said: 'Fidel, we can afford to pay them any price they ask. Because those bonds, in reality, won't be worth anything!' This brought much laughter.

"Fidel Castro puffed on his cigar thoughtfully. 'For the present, we may have to pay money for the cattle we take from them. We already have all the cattle ranches in Camagüey, but by the end of this year the state must control all the herds in Cuba. Pino Santos is now working on a plan whereby, in one fell swoop, all the cattle in the eastern provinces will come into our hands.' (Not long after, as I was preparing to resign my post in Zone 0-22, that order from Pino Santos arrived.)

"But now, Pino Santos objected to paying money for the herds. 'Fidel, couldn't we pay half in money and half in bonds in order to save something?' Castro roared with laughter. 'Don't be afraid, Pino,' he said. 'Soon the Cuban peso will be exactly like Ché's bonds—worth exactly nothing! We will have new money—corn pesos, coffee pesos, rice pesos!'

"There was much discussion of the cooperatives, and it was obvious that most of the delegates were having trouble putting over the idea with the *guajiros* who had been led to believe that they would own their own land. Fidel was very explicit: 'The land must belong to the state, not to the people,' he said. 'But you can't tell the *guajiros* that or they will become violent.'

"Someone suggested that it might be easier if the peasants were allowed to elect the administrator of the cooperative, or even be taught to administer it themselves. Castro vetoed the suggestion emphatically. 'The administrator of the cooperative must always be an INRA employee,' he declared. 'The *guajiro* has no capacity for administering, and if you let him elect the administrator, he will ruin the cooperative. You can't teach the *guajiro* to administer the cooperative because that would take years. It is first necessary for him to learn what we want him to learn. He must be taught the spirit of cooperation. He must lose what individualism he has and also this stupid passion for private property.'

"Fidel admitted that lots of problems were involved in the cooperative, one of which was the necessity of limiting the *guajiro's* earnings. 'If you limit his earnings, then they will say that the state is setting a maximum wage. Furthermore, the *guajiros* have been told that the total earnings of the cooperative will be divided among its members.'

"Ché Guevara said impatiently: 'Never mention that word *wages!* If you do you only disclose that the *guajiro* is now working for the state. Keeping on saying *limited earnings,* and tell the *guajiros* that the *total earnings* of the cooperative will be divided among them—eventually.'

"Guevara closed the meeting by repeating, only more baldly, the warning we had heard earlier from Núñez Jiménez.

" 'Remember,' said Ché, 'that you must never repeat outside this room anything that is discussed here. Get used to the fact that, at these meetings, we talk about *what we are going to do,* and not what we tell the people we are going to do. These are seldom the same thing.' "

Dr. Manuel Artime* emerged from that meeting shaken. But he had seen, at last, the real nature of the Cuban revolution, undisguised, naked, terrifying. Now the real motivation, the driving passion, behind Fidel Castro's verbose, fuzzy, contradictory public performance became painfully clear. The people had to be anesthetized because Cuba had to die in order for the new Communist Cuba to be born—with hunger, as Fidel said, acting as the midwife.

* Manuel F. Artime later became civilian chief of the Cuban Liberation Army, and was taken prisoner in the ill-fated invasion of April 1961. His account of the Castro conspiracy, *Traicion!* (Treason!), was published by Editorial Jus, S. A., Mexico City.

# Part Three

# THE AWAKENING

Chief source of the disturbing rumors of creeping communism which reached the people in the spring of 1959 was the rebel army and other branches of the armed forces. Beginning in January, the indoctrination of troops (which Nino Díaz first witnessed in the Sierra Maestra) was placed on a systematic basis. Raúl Castro, Minister of the Armed Forces, appointed as "Cultural Director" the well-known Communist, Osmani Cienfuegos, brother of Camilo Cienfuegos, chief of staff of the Revolutionary Army; schools were set up for senior officers (majors and captains), and political "instructors" became integral parts of military organizations down to the squad level.

"Among veteran officers of the rebel army," says Dr. Jorge Castellanos, "the objectives of this training were immediately obvious. They were, first, to weed out the officers who were anti-Communist or 'unreliable' from the Communist viewpoint; second, to indoctrinate those who could be trusted with troops or to prepare them for other jobs where they could be useful. However, even so-called 'reliable' men who were over thirty were not wanted in the new revolutionary armed forces. Younger and more pliable men were preferred as officers. The old rebel army was being liquidated. The more politically reliable officers were given jobs in the government, chiefly as administrators of INRA."

Juan Ramírez, a young university student whose previous military experience had been in the DRE (Students' Revolutionary Directorate) underground, joined the Revolutionary Air Force early in 1959. As a licensed civilian flier he was given accelerated training as a military pilot and would soon become an instructor.

"I was stationed at the San Antonio de los Baños base in Havana," he says, "with a group of about thirty cadets ranging in age from twenty to twenty-five. Most of the instructors were Chileans; they were good fliers but they were all Communists. Several were close friends of Ché Guevara who, we understood, had brought them to Cuba.

"We followed a stiff schedule from dawn to midnight, with breaks only at mealtime. As much time was spent in classrooms as on the drill field or in the hangars and in the air. The indoctrination was mostly lectures on history, politics, economics—all from the Marxist-Leninist standpoint. But there were also frequent oral quizzes or examinations, and that was when you had to be careful.

"These examinations followed a strange but rigid pattern. The instructor would ask a question and one of the Communists who were planted in every class would always be the first on his feet with the 'correct' Marxist answer. This served the purpose of giving the docile and ambitious students the 'line' to follow. But it also served to prod those who disagreed with the Communist approach into giving answers that were revealing to the instructor. For example, I remember a time when the question concerned the economic philosophy behind the agrarian reform. The correct answer was 'democratic socialism.' But one student said that it was Marxist-Leninist communism.

" 'Cadet, do you know what you are talking about?' the instructor asked.

" 'Yes sir,' the cadet answered. 'I have read the law and I recognize it as communism.'

"Later, that boy was called to the commandant's office. He was questioned for twenty-four hours, and then confined to quarters where he spent all his time with special tutors. He never came back to the squadron. We heard that he had a nervous breakdown and was discharged.

"The discharge rate was terrific; only a small percentage of those who enlisted were graduated as pilots. But there were lots of young men who wanted to be airmen, so the authorities could afford to get rid of all except the politically reliable. I managed to graduate because I was a good flier and I knew when to keep my mouth shut."

The Communist indoctrination of the armed forces was no closely guarded secret. Disgruntled or anti-Communist officers and washed-out cadets talked about it, and their families and friends passed the word, however discreetly. But for most Cubans it remained hearsay and rumor until the summer of 1959. Then it erupted in several national scandals that rocked the Castro regime and forced Cubans, at last, to face up to the Communist conspiracy.

### *The First Alarm*

On the morning of June 29, 1959, Major Pedro Díaz Lanz, commander-in-chief of the Revolutionary Air Force, was in bed recovering from a siege of typhus, when a visitor informed him that he was to be supplanted as chief. The reason was plain: before taking to his sick bed Díaz Lanz, like many other rebel army veterans, had complained to Fidel Castro about the Communist infiltration of the armed forces. "But I had gone one step further," says Díaz Lanz. "I had issued an order discontinuing all indoctrination classes in the Air Force. Fidel was furious."

Díaz Lanz got out of bed, dressed, and went to see Castro. "When I arrived," he says, "Fidel turned his back and left the room. I could only assume that reports of my dismissal were correct."

However, Díaz Lanz issued a statement to the press saying that he had returned from sick leave and was resuming his command. He stated that a rumor was being circulated that he had been a prisoner. "I wish to make it clear that we revolutionists were prisoners only under the Batista dictatorship, and that such a thing could not happen under a democratic regime." Then he added, pointedly: "I am against every type of dictatorship, including the most inhuman system in the world, communism."

Fidel Castro sent for him and demanded: "How dare you talk to the press like that?"

"Have I done wrong?" Díaz Lanz asked. "I only denied that I was a prisoner, and I said that I am opposed to communism. What is wrong with that?"

"Pedro, I order you to go to your home," said Castro. "We will decide what to do with you later."

Major Díaz Lanz went to his home, but only to write a letter to President Urrutia resigning from the service. "Actions against me," he wrote, "are due exclusively to the fact that I have always opposed an attitude which permits Communists to take prominent positions within the rebel army and within departments of the government. . . . Communist elements also have exerted pressure to carry out a certain plan of indoctrination [within the armed forces]. We all know, Mr. President, who they are, where they are, and what aims they pursue."

Then Díaz Lanz slipped aboard a boat with his wife, brother and several friends. When they were safely within the United States he made even more startling disclosures. Once, he said, while piloting Castro's private plane, he heard Fidel boast: "I am going to introduce in Cuba a system like the Russians have, only our Cuban system will be even better than the Russian system."

Basilio Martí, now a leader in the anti-Castro underground, was a government official at the time of Díaz Lanz's defection. "President Urrutia called Díaz Lanz a deserter and a traitor," he says, "but in this statement he also declared that he too was opposed to the Communist ideology. Raúl Castro heard of this and had the statement recalled. When it was re-issued the reference to communism had been deleted.

"Almost immediately the Communist press started a campaign against the President. Urrutia was a rather weak character, but he was basically a good man. He knew that Fidel was using him as a front, and he could see now the handwriting on the wall. Many of us began to admire him because there were signs that he was determined to go down fighting. He appeared on television with Luis Conte Agüero, the political commentator [a close friend of Fidel's who was already campaigning against the Communists], and made some strong anti-Communist statements while praising Castro.

"Fidel heard the broadcast and was furious at Urrutia. 'To hell with all this talk about communism,' he shouted. 'I'll give Cuba back to the reactionaries and let *them* fight the Communists!' What he meant by this became apparent a few days later when he made his big grandstand play and 'resigned' as Premier."

Castro's resignation was announced on the morning of July 17. That night, while Urrutia was virtually a prisoner in the presidential palace, Castro appeared on television and savagely attacked the President. "He is blackmailing us with communism," he screamed. "Everyone who promotes this ghost of communism is promoting foreign aggression. The President is drawing up a plan exactly like Díaz Lanz. Maybe he will send for fifteen North American agents and install them as his cabinet ministers."

Says Basilio Martí: "Fidel's scheme worked perfectly. The mobs threatened to hang Urrutia, and begged Fidel not to resign—all this, of course, was carefully staged. Urrutia was a defeated, broken man. He resigned as President while Castro was still on the air, and later escaped to the Venezuelan Embassy. Fidel reconsidered and withdrew his own resignation. The new President already had been chosen—Osvaldo Dorticós Torrado, a party hack who had been serving as Minister of Revolutionary Laws.

"Castro immediately launched a campaign against 'counter-revolutionaries,' principally in Oriente and Las Villas provinces. His fears were not entirely unfounded. The anti-Castro movement was beginning to take shape, although slowly. The Cuban people, generally, needed a few more jolts to make them open their eyes."

### *Hubert Matos Resigns*

Shortly after dawn on October 21, 1959, Camilo Cienfuegos, chief of staff of the Revolutionary Army, arrived at Agramonte Barracks in Camagüey and went directly to the quarters of Major Hubert Matos, military commander and INRA chief of the province. Señora María Luisa Araluce de Matos answered the doorbell and found the early caller impatient and upset. "I must see Hubert immediately," he insisted. Then, as he started up the staircase to Matos' study, he paused and said jovially: "María Luisa, it would be wonderful if you favored us with some of your superb *café oriental.*"

Señora de Matos went to prepare the coffee, puzzled and worried. She knew that on the preceding day Hubert Matos had sent in his resignation as army commandant and INRA official, which had pleased her enormously. Having distinguished himself in the rebel army as a soldier, administrator and agrarian reformer, her husband had earned the right to retire to their home in Manzanillo. Moreover, he was now embroiled in a hopeless struggle with the Camagüey Communists. What was the meaning of this sudden visit from their good friend, Cienfuegos? She was sure that trouble was afoot.

When she approached the door of Matos' study with

the coffee tray she overheard snatches of a disturbing conversation.

"Look around and see for yourself, Camilo," she heard her husband say. "You will find everything calm and peaceful at Agramonte. These reports of sedition and an uprising must be part of a scheme to get rid of me."

She could not hear Camilo's reply, but her husband said, "My revolutionary principles would never permit me to conspire against the government. That charge is ridiculous. My only purpose is to take María Luisa back to Manzanillo and live a peaceful life."

"Hubert, I am convinced of your innocence," Cienfuegos replied. "I beg you not to worry. I will straighten out this matter with Fidel."

"But you should not have interfered in this affair, Camilo," Matos said. "What I have done is my own responsibility. Fidel's reaction was to be expected. But now I am afraid that you will be his next victim."

Meanwhile, in the main office of the headquarters building, a group of officers was listening to a broadcast of the local radio which was vilifying Major Hubert Matos as a traitor and spreading the report that the Ninth Column which he commanded was the core of a new counterrevolutionary army. "We must strike while there is still time," said the broadcaster, "while we can still drag the rats out of the holes."

The listening officers were indignant and angry. "The whole thing was worked up by two Communist captains, Jorge Enrique Mendoza and Orestes Varela, and this Varela was doing the broadcasting," says one of Matos' lieutenants. "This was ridiculous, but it was getting dangerous too. The treason charge against Matos really started with a speech he had made on Lawyers' Day, June 8, in which he vigorously denounced the Communist infiltration of the government and the army. After that rebel army officers all over Cuba who shared his views or were having trouble with the Communists came to Hubert Matos, and he conscientiously reported the trouble directly to Fidel, who was his good friend. The most recent incident concerned Major Félix Duque in Oriente who had got into a squabble with the Communists. Castro had relieved Duque of his command and Matos had interceded for him. Now they were saying that all these men were in a conspiracy with Hubert Matos."

While the broadcast was going on, Camilo Cienfuegos suddenly appeared in the room with several aides. Those present agree that he was furious. "Turn that off," he ordered. "Captain, call that station immediately and tell them to stop the broadcast. If they don't obey, put them under arrest."

Cienfuegos remained only long enough to question the officers about conditions at Agramonte Barracks. He departed, saying that he was flying directly back to Havana to report to Castro.

"But right outside the headquarters," the lieutenant reports, "Camilo came face to face with Fidel Castro! We heard later that Fidel did not trust Cienfuegos to handle the Agramonte crisis, and had followed in his own plane. They walked a short distance and then stood talking. Camilo spoke quietly, earnestly, as if pleading with Fidel. But Fidel was blustering and gesticulating; in one angry outburst he said something about 'the plan has gone too far, there is no turning back.' Then he turned and walked away."

Later that morning the nine hundred officers and men of Agramonte Barracks were assembled on the drill field—surrounded by other contingents of the army which had been sent to Camagüey "to restore order." Castro, in a speech relayed throughout Cuba, announced that Major Hubert Matos had been relieved of his command and placed under arrest. He accused Matos of treason, inciting rebellion, and conspiring with Urrutia, Díaz Lanz, Batista and even the Dominican dictator Trujillo. "This was absurd, of course," says the lieutenant. "But what really astonished us was that Castro forced Camilo Cienfuegos to make a half-hearted statement supporting his charges against Matos."

Dr. Félix Barrera, who knew Hubert Matos intimately, was in the mob gathered outside the gates of Agramonte. "Since early morning," he says, "the inflammatory broadcasts had all of Camagüey City in an uproar. The troops sent in by Castro made a great show of 'securing' the key points of the city. Then, on his way from the airport Castro stopped his car repeatedly and told the crowds that he had come to put down a rebellion. Instead of putting down a rebellion he seemed to be inciting riots.

"Yet I am sure that many who were in that mob outside the gates that morning would have fought if necessary to save Hubert Matos, just like his own troops. They didn't believe Castro's ridiculous charges. They respected, even adored Matos, and knew that he was a Cuban patriot, a good Christian, not only a scholar but a real agriculturist, whose only 'rebellion' was trying to stop the Communists in their crazy, destructive program of agrarian reform. But that was another thing Castro had against Matos—he didn't like the people to idolize anyone but Fidel!"

## *The Voice of Matos*

While Castro was ranting on the drill field, Hubert Matos, confined to his quarters and under guard, sat down with a tape recorder and dictated a final statement. The tape was later entrusted by Señora de Matos (who is still in Cuba) to Francisco Lorié Bertot, the frail, venerable, courageous lawyer who undertook the impossible task of defending Matos at the subsequent "trial." These words are taken from that tape:

"My letter of resignation, which spoke frankly about the

real problem of communism, has motivated an inconceivable answer from Fidel, a man we believed to be honorable. He has stigmatized me as a traitor and counterrevolutionary. God forbid! . . .

"We fought against a regime of terror, oppression, torture, shame. Must we now accept these same things applied in the name of the revolution and against loyal men? How have we come to such abominable ways after 20,000 heroic dead, after so many sacrifices, after so many women's tears, after so much struggle and battle? That it now is being done in the name of the revolution, and by men in whom the people believe, because people still believe in Fidel, is more than saddening. It is lamentable, really, to be alive to see this happen.

"Well, Fidel, I am waiting, unperturbed, for whatever you command. Certainly, you know me well enough to know that I have the courage to face a firing squad serenely, or to spend a lifetime in prison, if that is what you decide. While you were in Camagüey today commanding them to seize the airport, the radio stations, the police headquarters in order to simulate an uprising which you could say I provoked, I had the courage to stay quietly here in my house with my wife and children, waiting for you to complete your crime. Those things were done just as you ordered. If this is what I deserve, so be it.

"I did not order my soldiers, our comrades from the Sierra, to fire against any Cuban, because they are not *my* soldiers! They are the soldiers of Cuba, of the Fatherland, of the revolution. I would not have them shoot even those despicable [Communists], the lowest of the low, that you sent here to create this trouble. They do not deserve shooting, they deserve something more. History will judge them, Fidel, just as history will one day judge you. Remember, Fidel, that men pass on. But history remembers their deeds, and history hands down the final verdict.

"Once, Fidel, you trusted the people; when you rebelled

against tyranny you called upon them to rise in the name of justice and reason, and they responded. Now, Fidel, you are destroying your work. You are burying the revolution.

"Perhaps there is some hope left. I appeal to you as a former comrade-in-arms, I appeal to the honor you used to have, not to save myself from prison or the firing squad, but to help save the revolution which belongs to the people. What else can you say to those who died for a better Cuba? What was the revolution fought for? Was it fought for intrigue? Was it fought for the corruption of men? No, Fidel, we fought for truth, for the high principles upon which civilization is founded. . . .

"Remember that much more even than the destiny of Cuba rests upon this revolution. A whole continent is watching, waiting, hoping to see [in our revolution] the way to a better future. . . .

"It does not matter whether I am imprisoned or buried in the ground. I shall be buried either way, in life or in death. One man's future matters little compared to the future of a people. Your own future does not matter, but the future of Cuba does. . . . This revolution is mine; I defended it, I believe in it, and I have the right to tell you these things and then take whatever comes along. Branded as a traitor, despised, changed to ashes, I will still say to you, Fidel, do not destroy the revolution!"

### *Camilo Disappears*

On October 22, 1959, Commandante Hubert Matos and thirty-eight of his officers and men were taken to Havana and imprisoned in Morro Castle to await trial. A week later the government announced that Camilo Cienfuegos and pilot, flying in a twin-engine Cessna, had disappeared mysteriously while on a routine flight from Camagüey to Havana. Fidel Castro personally assumed command of the armed forces assigned to the much-publicized land-air-sea search. No trace of the plane was ever found. Castro later enshrined Camilo Cienfuegos as one of the fallen heroes of the revolution.

Solution of the mystery, in all details at least, will have to await the liberation of Cuba; however, there is evidence that Cienfuegos was not "lost" but murdered by Fidel Castro in order to get the popular and romantic rebel out of the way before the Matos case came to trial.

"Camilo Cienfuegos was not aboard that plane," says Dr. Lorié Bertot, Matos' lawyer. "And the plane itself was never lost. At the time of the reported incident Camilo's dead body was somewhere in or near Havana.

"Castro knew, or had been warned by Raúl, that he might be making a martyr of Hubert Matos. This certainly would have been true if Camilo had testified for him, because they both were popular figures. So they did away with Cienfuegos and then made him a hero in order to offset the martyrdom of Matos."

## *The Matos Trial*

When Hubert Matos entered the theater of Camp Columbia (ironically renamed Ciudad Libertad) where the trial was held, at least four hundred rebel army men in the audience rose to their feet and cheered. Matos, surprised and embarrassed, motioned to them to be seated. During the recess, the four hundred were arrested; Fidel Castro called them "degenerates and traitors." Forty officers, denounced as instigators of the demonstration, had their beards shorn off and were banished to the interior.

The trial began on December 9, 1959, and lasted for six days. Fidel Castro took the stand and made a propaganda speech that ran on for six hours and was directed to the gallery and the television audience. "The guilt of these accused has been completely proven," he declared. "If they are acquitted, then history will condemn this tribunal."

"Raúl Castro allowed himself to be called as a witness for the prosecution," says Dr. Lorié Bertot. "He offered no evidence against Matos; his entire testimony was a tirade of insults, name-calling and bitter hatred of Hubert Matos. When I showed him three letters he had written to Matos in late 1958 praising his revolutionary record and congratulating him on his promotion to commander, Raúl turned on me and accused me of collaboration with the Batista government. Then he refused to be questioned further and left the stand."

Hubert Matos testified only briefly, but his testimony created a furor.

"Was there Communist infiltration in the army?" the prosecutor asked.

"Yes, it started during the last months of the war."

"But does this constitute a menace?"

"Yes, it constitutes a menace to a democratic regime in Cuba. Communists do not need a majority in order to gain power. History has proved this. I told Fidel about these things privately. It was he who made my charges public."

"Do you allow Communists to participate in Camagüey?"

"In Camagüey we tolerate them, because we are forced to; but we try not to allow them to participate any more than we have to."

"Was Commander Cienfuegos a Communist?"

"Camilo was not a Communist. He even appeared on the television in Camagüey and stated that there were Communists in the government."

"Why did you decide to resign your commission?"

"For various personal reasons, but mainly because I disagreed with the direction in which the revolution was being slanted. . . . My actions have always conformed to the ideology of the 26th of July Movement, and I have always expressed my opposition to communism."

Hubert Matos was found guilty of treason and ("in the generous spirit of the revolution which applies the maximum penalty only when the security and stability of the nation are threatened") was sentenced to twenty years imprisonment. The officers arrested with him were found guilty of "collaboration" or "sedition" and sentenced to prison terms ranging from two to seven years. Fourteen of them escaped from Morro Castle in October 1960 with the aid of guards who were navy men opposed to Castro.

"So far as we know," says Dr. Lorié Bertot, "Hubert Matos is still alive in the prison on the Isle of Pines. At first, Señora María Luisa, his wife, was allowed to visit him once a month, but this privilege was withdrawn in 1961. His aged father, who is in poor health, went to the Isle of Pines and begged to be allowed to see Hubert—'even if only from a distance'—before he died. The request was denied.

"This is the last message Hubert Matos gave me: 'If I die I hope my sacrifice will serve to alert the Cuban people and make them see the forces that menace their liberty and overshadow their destiny. Our principles and ideals cannot be destroyed, not even by death itself.' "

## *Castro Makes a Martyr*

Hubert Matos may be a controversial figure in Cuba's future. There are people in Camagüey—and Camagüeyans in exile—who despise him as heartily as they do Fidel and Raúl Castro. They claim to have known Matos while he was INRA chief of Camagüey, and they insist that he was a radical, a ruthless agrarian reformer, an excessively ambitious man who fell out with Fidel Castro politically. However, they are far outnumbered by those who, having known him well also, consider him one of the great heroes of the anti-Castro movement. Most Cubans, indeed, are convinced that the indictment and trial of Hubert Matos served to jolt the public into horrified realization of the Communist menace.

"That is the effect it had on me," says Dr. Luis Benítez, the psychiatrist, "as well as on my patients and most of my friends. I never knew Matos personally. I had heard from people who did know him that he was a leftist, a socialist, maybe even a Communist. But I found this hard to believe after his open, self-sacrificing denunciation of the Communists. I think he was another blind, passionate follower of Fidel Castro who experienced the bitter disillusionment.

"That is what made his indictment of the Communist danger so shocking and convincing. The Díaz Lanz charges, the degradation of President Urrutia, and all the rumors and suspicions now took on greater significance. Where we had closed our eyes to such things, now we opened them and began looking for evidence."

Says one of Matos' officers: "Even while we were imprisoned in Morro Castle we were aware that Hubert Matos had brought the Cuban people to their senses. We knew that the rebel army was too far gone to be saved. We doubted that the 26th of July Movement was strong enough now to survive the overwhelming Communist infection. But elsewhere there was still strength and hope—in the anti-Communist forces in labor, the universities, the church, and what was left of the free press."

Yet the Communist subversion of these Cuban institutions was farther advanced than he and his fellow inmates suspected. Most Cubans believed, for example, that by the end of 1959 the strongly anti-Communist labor movement had fought and won a spectacular battle against Red domination. What had actually happened, as they would soon discover, was that Fidel Castro, with the connivance of Brother Raúl and his Communist advisors, had already delivered the Cuban Confederation of Labor (CTC) into the hands of the Communist Party.

*The Assault on Labor*

During the spring of 1959 the thirty-three federations that comprised the Cuban Confederation of Labor elected delegates to the CTC congress scheduled for November. When the votes were counted the tally showed that the anti-Communists had won an overwhelming victory. Of the thirty-three unions, twenty-eight elected solidly anti-Communist delegations; only three went Communist, and the remaining two named delegations that were divided. The balloting in Cuba's largest union, the Federation of Sugar Workers, showed that only eight of the 243 locals were Communist-controlled.

"With this clear-cut evidence," says Carlos Rodríguez Quesada, CTC chief in Las Villas province, "our council prepared a report which was critical of Communist attempts to dominate the government, the army and the labor movement. David Salvador, the provisional head of the CTC, took a copy of this report to Castro. He warned Fidel that the congress would certainly condemn the Communists by a big vote, and probably would call upon Castro to make good on his promises to support a democratic labor movement.

"Fidel then called the five provincial secretaries of the CTC, of which I was one, to Havana for consultation. I don't know what he told the others, but when he found out that I was unalterably opposed to the Communists Castro said that he agreed with me. The Communists were trouble-makers, he said, and we had to get rid of them. He told me to go back to Las Villas and keep up the good work. However this was just one of his tricks.

"Shortly after I returned to Las Villas I received a call from Captain Alonso, the deputy commander of the army in the province, who had worked closely with me in the anti-Batista underground. He told me that he had received orders from Castro personally to investigate my anti-Communist activities, and he urged me to be careful. I went directly to David Salvador and told him what had happened. I also warned him that Castro was planning some kind of maneuver to prevent us from getting control of the CTC.

"Salvador, who is now in prison, has been accused of many things but he was never a Communist. He was really an anti-Communist socialist. His failing was his complete faith in Fidel Castro. At any rate, he told me to go right ahead with our organization work. 'Don't worry,' he said, 'I will make things right with Fidel.'

"The CTC congress opened on November 18, 1959. Although the Communists had only about 150 out of the 3,000 delegates present, they maneuvered their people into key positions on various committees and the auditorium was patrolled by pro-Communist militiamen. The first all-night session broke up in a riot when they tried to get three well-known Communists elected to the executive committee."

Castro's declaration that the revolution was "not red but olive green" had inspired a typically Cuban rejoinder. "The revolution is really like a melon," people said, "green outside, red inside!" So, as part of the demonstrations, many delegates had brought to the convention hall watermelons which they held aloft while chanting "*Melones! Melones!*" in defiance of the Communists.

Rodríguez Quesada continues: "When the fighting started it was a question of whether there were more broken heads than broken melons. Actually, I believe Castro wanted this fight to take place. He knew that if there was a real election of officers the Communist candidates would be defeated by a tremendous vote.

"Now he made a dramatic appearance to restore order.

He said the place looked like a lunatic asylum. Then he made his impassioned appeal for 'unity,' by which he meant a coalition of Communists and others. He said that the labor movement 'must not become the knife in the heart of the revolution.'

"When he finished his two-hour harangue, he sent for David Salvador. 'David, are you for or against unity?' he asked. Salvador didn't like the idea at all. But he always went along with Fidel. So he said he was for unity. 'Very well,' said Fidel. 'Go tell your people to vote for the unity ticket which now will be introduced. If you do this you will get a vote of confidence and be elected president of the CTC.'

"Castro produced the list of officers, directors and committee members. He made it plain that only these people would be acceptable. There would be a single ticket and no opposition. Many of the people he named were unknowns, but we soon discovered that they were secret Communists or sympathizers. These were the real '*melones*.'

"Who conceived this plan? Not Fidel. The maneuver was planned for him by Raúl Castro who had the advice of Lázaro Peña, the Communist who had headed the first CTC under Batista. People said that Fidel had even worked the miracle of resurrecting Lazarus, because Lázaro Peña eventually was installed again as the head of the Communist-controlled CTC."

The Communist campaign to purge the labor movement of democratic leaders began immediately after the November convention. The same tactics were employed in most cases: the Communist press would begin a campaign of slander against the victim; a special assembly of the CTC would be called to hear the charges; then the leader would be ousted in a rigged election.

Says Rodríguez Quesada: "Salvador complained bitterly

to Castro about what was happening. Castro's answer was always one of painful regret, and a plea for David to be patient. Fidel said that if it were not for the difficulties he was having with the U.S., he would kick the trouble-making Communists out of the labor movement. He promised that as soon as the Yankees left him alone he would do that. This was shrewdly calculated to quiet Salvador, who was always strongly anti-American.

"But Castro knew he had to get Salvador out of the way. So early in 1960 he sent David on a mission to France. While Salvador was gone the purge reached a climax; when he got back in March the leaders of twenty-two of the twenty-eight democratic federations had been deposed. Salvador flew into a rage and resigned as head of the CTC. He went underground shortly thereafter and began forming the anti-Communist '30th of November Movement.' Then, on November 5, 1960, Salvador was arrested with several confederates and charged with trying to leave Cuba illegally and with the 'illegal' possession of $13,000 which he was taking to some underground leaders in exile. He has been in a dungeon in La Cabaña Fortress ever since. In March 1961 he led an uprising of prisoners and was severely beaten by the guards. We know that his collarbone was broken by a blow from a rifle butt."

## *Leader of the Lost Cause*

Amaury Fraginals, head of the powerful Federation of Electrical Workers, was one Cuban labor leader who was determined to fight the Communists to the bitter end. Early in January 1959, after being released from La Cabaña where he had served a term as an anti-Batista saboteur, Fraginals was elected general secretary of the traditionally anti-Communist federation. But he found himself handicapped by the opposition of five Communists who had won places on the twelve-man executive board.

Fraginals' first action after taking office was to negotiate a new contract with the Cuban Power & Light Company which gave the workers salary increases amounting to $4,000,000 a year. Instead of rejoicing, the comrades in the union denounced Fraginals as a "traitor to the revolution" and demanded his expulsion from the union and the 26th of July Movement of which he was a leader.

"The reason for this," Amaury Fraginals explains, "was that the Communists already knew of the government's plans to confiscate the power company. Wages could be increased so long as private enterprise had to meet the payrolls; but to saddle the government with a four million increase amounted to treason!"

Fraginals took the issue to an open meeting of the federation and won an overwhelming vote of confidence from the members. But he was smart enough to see that he had won only one battle in a war that would go on. When the Federation of Electrical Workers met a few months later to elect delegates to the CTC congress, Fraginals was in the hospital undergoing treatment for a gastric ulcer, a hangover from prison days. He dressed and slipped out of the hospital and went to the Radio Cine Theater in downtown Havana where the meeting was being held.

"When I walked down the aisle," he says, "everybody stood up and cheered. I had been out of circulation for a month and there were rumors that I was through. Martínez Sánchez, the Minister of Labor, was furious. He had already put up his slate of delegates and expected to have them elected. I denounced his delegates, citing their Communist records, and introduced a ticket made up of our own people. We won such a smashing victory that Martínez Sánchez stalked off the platform swearing."

Fraginals returned to the hospital. His condition worsened, and on the day that the CTC congress opened he was under the surgeon's knife. When he came to and heard about Castro's successful "unity" maneuver he began yelling for his clothes and had to be restrained. Five days later he heard that a meeting of the anti-Communist labor leaders was taking place and managed to slip out of the hospital.

"This meeting," he says, "was attended by people from the twenty-eight federations which had sent anti-Communist delegations to the congress. We drew up a pledge stating that we would support any federation that was being attacked or infiltrated by the Communists. However, Fidel Castro had done his work too well. Only six of the federations represented had the courage to sign the pledge. I knew then that the cards were stacked against us, but I swore that the electrical workers would fight to the bitter end. I got the democratic members of our executive committee to sign a document pledging loyalty to me in the fight. We knew that the rank-and-file members were with us.

"From that time on we fought a running battle with our enemies. Things really got hot in August 1960 when, at a big rally in the Havana baseball park, Raúl Castro announced the confiscation of the Cuban Power & Light Company and all other public utilities. The Communist 'interventor' who took charge of the power company immediately began firing employees and promoting his own people. The purpose was to undermine our position in the union."

Fraginals again called a meeting of the federation and got from the membership a point-by-point denunciation of the interventor's tactics. Communist officers of the CTC who were seated on the dais objected violently and demanded that the matter be referred to the Ministry of Labor. Fraginals answered: "The matter already has been referred, point by point, to the members of this federation. You have heard their answers."

Next, Amaury Fraginals was called to the Ministry of Labor, where Martínez Sánchez warned him: "Fraginals, you are getting yourself in real hot water with Fidel. This is the last time you will be told to cease causing so much trouble."

"From that day on," says Fraginals, "I was dogged by G-2 men [secret police]. They followed my car everywhere, parked outside my house, and even trailed after me when I walked on the street. It got to be a joke. I would say to them: 'Why don't you ride in my car, or let me ride with you? Think how much gasoline we could save!' Then the propaganda started. I was denounced as a traitor, a counter-revolutionary, and accused of wrecking the labor unions. They put up posters vilifying me and telling lies about my record as a labor leader. I drew up my own posters setting the record straight, but I couldn't find a printer who dared to print them for me."

On November 30, 1960, saboteurs blew up five power terminals in Havana. Three nights later they raided the power company and stole $100,000, presumably for the anti-Castro underground. The CTC called a general meeting of electrical workers to be held on December 9 to "fix responsibility" for the sabotage and theft. Fraginals was ordered to appear personally.

Says Fraginals: "I knew that they intended to kick me out of the labor movement by charging me with responsibility for these incidents. So I rounded up our workers in small groups. 'We must appear at this meeting and defend our rights,' I told them. 'This is the last-ditch fight of the Communists to capture our union. The odds are against us, but we must go on fighting. They may send me to the wall, but we must not give up now.' I also called a press conference and told the whole story."

The crucial meeting was announced for 5:30 P.M. on December 9. Shortly after four o'clock Fraginals received word that over 5,000 people were trying to crowd into the union meeting-hall which would hold only 900. He sent word to have the meeting held outside the building.

"As I approached the building," he says, "four G-2 men grabbed me and shoved me into a car. Immediately a cry went up: 'Fraginals has been arrested!' Then the mob attacked the car, flattened the tires, and smashed in the hood. I managed to get out and climb up on top. 'Let us march to the palace,' I said, 'and ask Dorticós what rights they are trying to take from us now.' The crowds cheered. They lifted me to their shoulders and started toward the palace chanting, 'Cuba si! Rusia no!'

"I was absolutely flabbergasted by this demonstration, because not all these people were our members. They were Cubans blowing off their deep resentment of the regime. Our people were crying 'Elections! Elections!' They meant *union* elections, but the mob thought we meant national elections, so they took up the cry enthusiastically."

### *Labor's Last Stand*

The crowd reached the Malecón, turned right on Misiones Avenue and approached the northern terrace of the presidential palace. The militiamen, obviously frightened, closed ranks with their rifles ready. The demand for an audience with President Dorticós was sent inside; word came back that the President would receive Fraginals only if the crowds left the palace grounds.

"I ordered the crowd to disperse," says Fraginals, "but there were howls of protest. Our people warned me not to go in alone, or I would be arrested. 'Lead everybody back to our building,' I told them. 'If I don't join you there within an hour, come and get me.' Then I was amazed to see how the mob obeyed. They left singing and shouting, and marched to our building, which was some distance away."

Fraginals was accompanied into the palace by three union officers and his sister-in-law, a popular woman who had fought in the Sierra Maestra. They were received by Dorticós, Labor Minister Martínez Sánchez and a number of aides.

"Dorticós asked angrily what I thought I was doing by causing so much trouble for the revolutionary government," Fraginals recalls. "I told him we were not fighting against the Cuban revolution, but against the Communist revolution. He accused me of being a demagogue and of taking away the rights of the workers. I pointed to Martínez Sánchez. 'There is the man who is taking away the workers' rights,' I said. 'He is a Communist, and the Communists are destroying the labor movement. And now I am speaking not for myself but for those thousands of people who brought me here.'

"Just then an aide came in and handed Dorticós several long sheets from a teletype machine. He turned pale. 'Listen to what you have done, Fraginals,' he said. Then he began to read from the AP-UPI [Associated Press and United Press International] accounts of my press conference. When he had finished he told me angrily that I had besmirched the revolution in the eyes of the whole world. He demanded that I give a statement to Prensa Latina [the official news agency] denying that I had said such things. I refused flatly. Then I looked at my watch. 'I have been here almost an hour,' I said. 'The crowd will come back for me soon and you will have further trouble.' He urged me to telephone our headquarters and say that the conference was continuing. Then he asked me what I wanted.

"I told him we wanted the terms of our contract respected, and no more firing, hiring, or demotions by the interventor. I said we wanted new elections held without interference from the government or the CTC. If this was not done, I said, our federation was determined to pull out of the CTC altogether. Dorticós turned to Martínez Sánchez and told him to see that our demands were answered. Then once again he took up the AP-UPI dispatches. He practically begged me for the statement. I said I must have time to think it over. Then I left the palace and went to our headquarters. The crowd was still there, but I told them everything was settled and urged them to go home.

"Inside, I called a meeting and told my colleagues how things really stood. They urged me not to give Dorticós his statement. They were convinced that all was lost, and that Martínez Sánchez would never honor our demands."

Fraginals stalled for forty-eight hours, then he received a warning that his arrest had been ordered. Five days later, in a hideaway, he sat in front of a television set and watched a packed meeting of the CTC, with Fidel Castro on the platform, purge him and the other democratic leaders from the Cuban labor movement. The charges against them were immediately answered in handbills from an underground printing press.

The G-2 went into action. Orders were issued to shoot Fraginals on sight. Photos taken of the December 9 march on the presidential palace were blown up and many of the demonstrators were identified and arrested.

"I managed to escape the dragnet for nearly a month," says Fraginals. "Each night I moved to a new hideout. But on the night of January 14, as I moved cautiously along the street, I spotted a G-2 car following me. When I started to run they opened fire. I pulled out a Luger I was carrying and managed to put a few shots through the windshield. Then I ran around the corner, stopped a car at gun point, and forced the driver to take me to an embassy. Of course, I had to stay there because it was impossible to get safe-conduct."

Toward the end of January 1961, Fraginals got restless. One night he slipped out of the embassy, and managed to elude the G-2 guards who were watching his asylum. By devious means, known only to the underground, he got to Mexico and, eventually, to the United States.

"Before 1959," says Amaury Fraginals, "organized labor in Cuba was one of the proudest examples of the democratic labor movement in the free world. Cuban workers received the highest wages in Latin America. They had guaranteed minimum wages, paid vacations, benefits for sickness and old age, the right to strike, job security and many benefits enjoyed by workers in only a few other countries.

"By the end of 1960, most of these benefits had been abolished—by a regime which claims to be creating a 'workers' republic.' Wages have been reduced, and take-home pay depleted further by 'voluntary contributions' withheld for agrarian reform, national defense and other 'patriotic' causes. Strikes are prohibited by law. Collective bargaining is unheard of. Overtime and paid vacations must be sacrificed 'in the interests of the people.' Service in the militia, without compensation, is compulsory."

Two years after the tragic CTC Congress of 1959, the Cuban Communists added a brazen postscript to the destruction of the free labor movement. At the Communist-dominated CTC Congress held in November 1961 (presided over by Lázaro Peña), Labor Minister Martínez Sánchez shouted defiantly: "Those rascals who opposed the unified labor movement and who stood in the aisles yelling '*melones! melones!*'—they are no longer here! But you are here! The '*melones*' are here! And we shall always be here, because we shall always be '*melones*'—green outside but red inside!"

## *Censorship by Terror*

Castro's desperate urgency to get control of the unions was motivated by more than the plan to nationalize industry. "His primary target," says Humberto Medrano, formerly of *Prensa Libre,* "was the free press, as well as Cuban radio and television. Communist experience made him and his cohorts aware of the fact that you cannot deceive the public so long as there are independent newspapers to publish facts and pinpoint lies. Hence, freedom of expression had to be abolished. But Fidel could not afford to repeat the Batista type of censorship. His tactics were much more ingenious."

Immediately after January 1, 1959, Castro ordered the confiscation of newspapers and radio-TV stations which had supported Batista or had been subsidized by the Batista regime. Five daily newspapers were taken over in Havana alone. "Many Cubans considered this proper," says Medrano. "However, much as they hated Batista and Batistianos, if they had looked closely at *how* Fidel killed off these papers they would have recognized the totalitarian tendency of the regime. These properties were seized by force. The plants and equipment were simply handed over to the Communists. There were no auctions or sales which might have allowed democratic interests which wished to start new papers to buy the confiscated presses and other equipment."

Castro went even further. The Communist newspapers, led by *Hoy* and *Revolución* (which posed as the "official organ of the 26th of July Movement"), were given exclusive access to all important news, including the new "revolutionary laws" which affected the lives of all Cubans. "Carlos Franqui, the former proofreader of *Hoy* who became editor of *Revolución,* and a few other government-favored newsmen, attended all cabinet meetings, and no other reporters were allowed," says Medrano. "*Revolución* participated in important police and military investigations. *Revolución* and *Hoy* were allowed to distribute in the provinces. They could even use military aircraft in their work. This, of course, put other newspapers at great disadvantage."

Humberto Medrano analyzes Castro's strategy in muzzling and eventually killing the free press: "Advertising and circulation revenue is the lifeblood of a newspaper. Castro resorted to economic strangulation of the press first by denying government advertising to all but the semi-official [Communist] newspapers, and secondly by intimidating private advertisers. Then he resorted to strong-arm methods to kill circulation by threatening distributors and dealers, wrecking and burning delivery trucks, and even inciting riots to scare off the public."

The revolutionary regime was little more than a month old when Castro exhibited his painful sensitivity to criticism. The weekly humor magazine, *ZigZag*, ran a cartoon mildly poking fun at Fidel's public performance. His reaction was a television tantrum in which he threatened to have *ZigZag* suppressed. In March 1959, *Prensa Libre* published a series of editorials asking for free elections and pointing to the Communist infiltration of the government. Castro appeared at a public meeting in Havana's Alameda de Paula angrily waving a copy of *Prensa Libre* and accusing publisher Sergio Carbó of "undermining the prestige of the revolution." The mob responded with hysterical cries of "*Paredón! Paredón!*" [The execution wall] for publisher Carbó.

Carbó replied with another editorial criticizing "mob justice" and adding that he would publish more editorials "since it is not yet a crime to complain." Castro returned to the attack the next day with another televised denunciation of Carbó. "What does Carbó mean?" Castro demanded. "Cuba *has* a free press!"

Next, the unions demanded—and were granted—the right to attach to any news story or editorial a *coletilla*, a footnote or comment which *Prensa Libre* described as an "impudent ending." The *coletillas* denied the facts, introduced Communist propaganda, and became increasingly abusive of the editors. They also grew longer and longer; *Diario de la Marina* (one of the oldest newspapers in the Western Hemisphere) began publishing a daily "box score" of *coletillas* vs. news in the Havana newspapers.

"Finally, I decided to find out who was writing these anonymous insertions in our newspaper," says Dr. José Ignacio Rivero, editor of *Diario de la Marina*. "This required no real detective work. When I finished writing or editing an article I would place it in the pneumatic tube which took it to the composing room. Then I would sit back and watch. Always the same man got up from his desk and left the news room. Shortly after he returned, the pneumatic tube would pop out the cylinder containing the proofs—with a scurrilous note set in type below the article.

"I was utterly amazed, because this man was one of my best friends! He had been with our paper for more than twenty years. Many times we had traveled in Europe together with our wives. I don't know if he ever became a Communist, but he was a left-winger and a rabid *Fidelista*. Finally he broke with the Castro regime; he is now, I think, an exile somewhere in Spain."

In July 1959 two new sections were added to the "Code of Social Defense" which gave the revolutionary government life-and-death powers over publications and broadcasting stations that criticized the regime. The penalties were confiscation of property plus sentences of imprisonment or death. Then the independent papers which were sharpening, rather than toning down, their criticism of communism and Castro were marked for the killing.

*Avance* was the first sizable daily to feel the axe. Says ex-publisher Jorge Zayas: "When the Castro forces were victorious in January 1959 I was elated. I thought it was a glorious day for Cuba. But when it became more and more apparent that Castro was carrying Cuba into a

Communist dictatorship, I began to protest editorially. Castro immediately resorted to the old Communist trick of 'censorship by terror.'

"In November 1959 I went to the United States to attend a journalism seminar, and while there I spoke frankly about conditions in Cuba. Castro was furious. While I was in Washington I went to the State Department; Castro charged that I had gone there to enter into some kind of conspiracy with the 'Yankee imperialists.' I replied that I had gone to the State Department along with fourteen other Latin American newspapermen. We had gone there not to conspire but to observe the operations of a foreign office—most of the others reported this in cables to their papers at home.

"When I arrived in Havana, I was detained and cross-examined in the airport. A few nights later Castro's policemen pounded on the door of my home. They were very polite and apologetic, and said they had come to investigate a 'stupid report' that I had a cache of arms hidden in my home. They searched the house and, of course, found nothing.

"Shortly before Christmas 1959 I had another clash with Castro. During a labor rally in Havana, David Salvador, the head of the CTC, demanded that *Avance* be confiscated and the editors shot. Fidel Castro then got up and supported Salvador's charges by saying that *Avance* was a dangerous newspaper and that I was a 'counter-revolutionary.' I knew that the end was in sight, so I sent my family out of Cuba. On January 18, 1960, members of the printers' union took over the plant and I was forced to flee the country."

*Excelsior* and *El País* were forced to close down in February 1960 after the printers' union demanded prohibitive wage increases as well as the right to approve editorials and censor the news. "Most of our employees were already members of the militia," says Guillermo Mártinez Márquez, former editor of *El País*. "So we had military units in our press room, business office and editorial rooms. These Trojan horse units were the shock troops always on the alert inside every newspaper plant."

About the same time, *El Mundo* was seized on the pretext that the publisher had been in "collaboration with Batista." Castro decided to bypass *Información*, which had dropped its editorial page entirely, because he knew he could deal with it later by economic strangulation. He now concentrated on his two severest critics, *Prensa Libre* and *Diario de la Marina*.

### *Death of the Free Press*

A bitter campaign of slander and vilification was launched against the publishers and editors of both papers in *Revolución* and *Hoy*. The loudest voice in the assault was that of radio commentator José Pardo Llada, who served as Castro's chief hatchetman until he himself was forced to flee Cuba.

"At the peak of this vicious campaign," says Humberto Medrano, "the staff of *Prensa Libre* drew up a statement pledging their support to the newspaper. This was signed by over eighty per cent of our editorial and mechanical employees. The day after it was published all employees were summoned to CTC headquarters. They were held there for seven hours, surrounded by militiamen, and thoroughly brainwashed. Then they were forced to repudiate their statement, and to sign another which 'endorsed the decisions of the Workers' Secretariat, to which we pledge an unlimited vote of confidence.'

"Then, at one o'clock in the morning, they were invited to meet Fidel Castro in the offices of *Revolución*. The relatively few who went there were told bluntly by Castro that 'workers must never side with their employers, no matter how well they are paid, because the employer is always the enemy of the workers.' "

The next victim, however, was not *Prensa Libre* but *Diario de la Marina.* "The attacks against us," says Editor Rivero, "by *Revolución* and Pardo Llada had become so vicious and so numerous by May 1960 that we knew Castro meant to destroy us. I too received a letter, which was signed by four hundred employees, pledging support and urging me to keep up the fight. However, I thanked them and put the letter in my pocket. I told them that they would only invite trouble for themselves if I published it.

"But some of the Communists in our shop reported the incident to union headquarters. A few days later militiamen appeared to solicit signatures to a statement which denounced me and the paper. Now I called our employees together and asked them for permission to publish their original statement. The spokesman replied 'We meant for you to publish it when we wrote it; now we urge you to do so.' I sent the letter to the composing room with orders to publish it in the next day's paper. This all happened during the morning of May 10, 1960.

"While I was having luncheon that day I received a telephone call urging me to come to the plant immediately. There I found twenty militiamen with hammers destroying the cylinder containing the letter. I ordered a new cyclinder made and placed on the press. That night I remained in the plant until I saw the presses begin to roll.

"But while I was out having dinner I received another phone call. 'They have come back and have stopped the presses,' I was informed. 'Now they are trying to persuade the employees to replace the cylinder.'

"When I drove up to our building, several employees were outside waiting for me. 'Do not go inside,' they warned. 'The militiamen are waiting to arrest you.' I told them to go back and tell the press-room crew that I wanted the letter printed and accompanied by a story telling what had happened that day.

"The next morning when the paper was delivered to me I saw that the letter had been killed. There were headlines on the front page of my own paper calling me a Fascist, a Yankee imperialist and other things. I got into my car and drove to an embassy and asked for asylum."

Seated in front of the embassy television set that evening, José Ignacio Rivero watched the mock funeral and burial of *Diario de la Marina.*

"The cameras followed the mob as it passed through Havana," he says. "The leaders carried a coffin which they carried to the 'grave' at the foot of the famous Alma Mater monument on the University of Havana campus. From the coffin they removed a dummy bearing my name, placed a rope around the neck, and hanged me in effigy. The dummy was cut down, placed back in the coffin, and *Diario de la Marina* was buried."

*Prensa Libre,* next on the list, decided to die fighting. "The day after the 'burial' of *Diario,*" says Medrano, "we ran an editorial entitled 'The Grave-Diggers.' In it we stated: 'It is painful to see freedom of thought and expression buried at our center of culture. It is almost like seeing the code of laws buried at a court of justice.'

"As we expected, *Revolución* opened fire immediately with an editorial headlined: 'The Treacherous Voice of *Prensa Libre.*' This was followed by several days of riots and demonstrations in front of our building with the usual demands of the firing squad (*'paredón, paredón!'*) for the Carbós and myself. For several nights our houses were under the surveillance of Castro's G-2 agents so we were unable to sleep at home.

"On Monday, May 16, the Communists among our employees appeared in the office with armed militiamen. The editor in charge was informed that the lead editorial and certain articles for that day's paper could not be published 'because they are subversive.' That afternoon, after we had refused to change or withdraw the articles, the newspaper was seized and we sought asylum in the embassy of Panama.

"Today the *Prensa Libre* building is occupied by the scurrilous *Revolución*, which is printed on our presses. Carlos Franqui, the Communist proofreader, occupies Ulises Carbó's office, and publisher Sergio Carbó's private office is reserved for Fidel Castro who comes in occasionally to enjoy his booty."

*Información* succumbed to Castro's economic squeeze on December 23, 1960. The InterAmerican Press Association mourned: "The last independent publication in Cuba has disappeared. From now on the people of that Communist-dominated island will be deprived of reading any news other than that which the government wants them to." Three months later, in March 1961, the IAPA reported to its semi-annual assembly in Acapulco, Mexico: "There is not even a glimmer of freedom in Cuba now."

## *Comrade Mikoyan Arrives*

The Sovietization of Cuba began in earnest with the arrival in Havana of Anastas I. Mikoyan, First Deputy Premier of the Soviet Union, in February 1960. The ostensible purpose of Mikoyan's visit was to open a Soviet industrial, cultural and scientific exhibition in Havana's Palace of Fine Arts. While he was in Cuba, however, Mikoyan signed a trade agreement whereby the USSR promised to buy five million tons of sugar (paying only twenty per cent cash, the balance in Soviet goods and equipment) and to grant Cuba a credit of one hundred million dollars plus technical assistance. This was followed by a resumption of diplomatic relations with Russia, Red China, the bloc countries, and by additional trade agreements with Poland, Czechoslovakia, East Germany and Communist China.

The fanfare over Cuba's new economic alliance with the Soviets drowned out some of the more ominous sounds of the Mikoyan performance. Dr. Emilio Maza, a Havana law professor who was then trying to cut his way through the jungle of new "revolutionary laws," noticed that "few Cubans seemed to have been listening carefully when Mikoyan, in one of his speeches, revealed the 'secret' of communizing an economy. He said that 'the secret lies in confiscating *without compensation* all sources of production, land, subsoil, forests, and turning all these riches over to their legitimate owners, the people.'

"The most radical measures adopted by the Castro government followed Mikoyan's remark. Laws were written and rewritten to enable the government to seize property without any compensation to the owner. Between March and October United States properties valued at over one billion dollars—public utilities, factories, sugar mills, ranches, banks, oil refineries, etc.—were taken outright. In October the assault on Cuban-owned property began with the passage of Law 890 which declared that it was the 'duty' of the government to nationalize industrial and commercial enterprises 'which did not and could never adapt themselves to the revolutionary reality of our country.' This was followed by the so-called Urban Reform Law which made tenants theoretically the owners of the property they occupied—although they were obligated to pay rent plus upkeep charges to the government which was now a sort of 'mortgage holder.'

"By the end of 1960 the Castro government had carried out the 'Mikoyan plan' in all aspects. There was no longer anything like private property in Cuba."

Dr. Herminio Portell Vilá, an authority on international communism, was startled by the number of Spaniards, many of whom he recognized, who came in the Mikoyan entourage. "There were over one hundred of them," he says, "some had come to Cuba as refugees after the Spanish Civil War and had returned to the Soviet Union following World War II. Others had been taken to the USSR as children. All spoke fluent Russian as well as Spanish. They were trained for specialized work in industry, government, and propaganda. Needless to say, they were all doctrinaire Communists.

"These 'Cuban' Spaniards were with Mikoyan when the Soviet exposition was on display in Mexico City. But the significant thing is that after the exposition closed in Havana these Spaniards remained in Cuba. They served as technicians, indoctrinators, propagandists. Of course, they fitted into Cuban life much more easily than the Communists from the Slavic countries.

"Those who came with Mikoyan, however, were merely an advance guard. As a result of arrangements he made, other Spanish Communists-in-exile began to arrive by the boatload. One outstanding addition, for example, was General Enrique Líster Forjan, the Asturian *dinamitero*, who acquired his rank in the Red Army and fought in the Spanish Civil War. His first job in Cuba was to set up the *vigilante* or 'neighborhood spy' system. He later became commander of the camp in Minas del Frío, in the Sierra Maestra, where Latin American Communists are trained in guerrilla warfare."

At the time of the Mikoyan visit, Dr. Nicolás Rivero, a former Cuban delegate to the Organization of American States, was an official in Castro's Ministry of Foreign Relations. "Mikoyan made arrangements," he says, "to send to Havana Alexei Alekseyev, chief of the Latin American section of the Kremlin Foreign Office. Alekseyev's mission was to curb the hot-heads, like Raúl Castro, and prevent them from doing anything that might enable the United States to intervene through the OAS.

"He also advised Castro to purge the Cuban foreign service of career officers who had served under the old regime, and to replace them with reliable but *unknown* Cuban Communists. Alekseyev repeatedly emphasized that it was dangerous to appoint well-known Communists to key positions in the government and particularly in the foreign service.

"Alekseyev was the most important of some seventy Soviet advisors who came to Cuba in 1960 as a result of the Mikoyan visit. He made arrangements also for Raúl Castro to visit Prague and Moscow that summer. While in Prague, Raúl made his bid for Cuba's admission to the Warsaw Pact—the Soviet counterpart of NATO. Khrushchev vetoed that proposal, but he did agree to send Castro military technicians and experts in guerrilla warfare to reorganize the Cuban military establishment."

## *Underground Voices*

While Comrade Mikoyan was in Cuba several incidents occurred which had unforeseen consequences. He placed a ceremonial wreath before the statue of the Cuban patriot, José Martí—and unwittingly launched a rugged and enduring element of the anti-Castro underground. The Soviet exposition also precipitated an open break between Fidel Castro and his long-time friend, Luis Conte Agüero, Cuba's popular political commentator; and Conte Agüero's defection marked the end of independent broadcasting in Cuba.

The wreath-laying incident occurred at noontime on February 5, 1960, in Havana's Parque Central. Says Juan Manuel Salvat, who was a student in the University of Havana at the time: "It was traditional for distinguished visitors to place a wreath before the statue of Martí. But when we learned that Mikoyan's wreath was a floral arrangement in the form of the Soviet flag with hammer and sickle, a group of about one hundred and fifty students decided to stage a counter-demonstration with a wreath bearing the Cuban flag.

"We arrived in Parque Central just as Mikoyan was laying his wreath. We marched toward the statue singing the national anthem and carrying placards which said: 'Fidel, sí—Comunismo, no!' The militiamen met us with leveled guns. They destroyed our wreath and then the shooting started. Twenty-one students were arrested. The five leaders, including Alberto Muller and myself, were expelled from the university. That was when we revived the Students' Revolutionary Directorate (DRE) which had fought against every dictatorship since Machado's. Alberto Muller became our leader. The last thing we did before going underground was to rally the university students against Castro's mobs and militiamen in defense of Luis Conte Agüero, the courageous anti-Communist, who was about to be crucified in Mikoyan's honor."

Castro's close friendship with Luis Conte Agüero began when both were students at the University of Havana. "Fidel was a remarkable fellow in those days," says Conte Agüero. "But he was a combination genius and juvenile delinquent; one moment he would show signs of brilliance, and the next he would behave like a hoodlum. I was interested, and I felt sorry for him. He could turn out to be a great leader, I thought, or else the worst type of gangster."

Conte Agüero was in close touch with Castro before the reckless assault on the Moncada Barracks, during Fidel's imprisonment and while he was in exile in Mexico. By the time Castro returned to Cuba and went into the Sierra, Conte Agüero had become Cuba's foremost political commentator. "Fidel and I had developed quite different ideas about which course the Cuban revolution should take," says Conte. "His ideas were much more radical than mine; but after the war with Batista started

I supported Castro. However, despite what Castro says now, I am positive that before 1960 he was not a Communist. I think he became a Communist solely because he wanted to maintain his power and not by the ideological route."

Early in 1959, Conte Agüero, whose previous work had been confined to radio and a newspaper column, joined CMQ-TV, Cuba's largest network, which was owned by the Mestre brothers and based in Havana's elaborate Radio-Centro. Radio-television in Cuba played a much larger role than the press in shaping public opinion. "Cubans believed first what they heard from their friends," says Alonso León, the soap salesman, "next what they heard on radio-TV, and last what they read in the press. But there is no doubt that Conte Agüero was one of the most listened-to political analysts in Cuba."

Fidel Castro favored his old friend Conte from the start. He provided him with credentials which stated that Luis Conte Agüero was a semi-official advisor; he took Conte Agüero with him on flying trips throughout Cuba and to South America; and, because Fidel never passed up a chance to talk over the TV networks, he appeared frequently on Conte's popular forty-five-minute telecast over CMQ. "Fidel would simply drop in whenever it suited him," says Conte. "I could not estimate how many times, but I know he always talked overtime, and once he even established a record. My program ran from 1:30 to 2:15 each afternoon. Fidel started talking one day at 1:30 and we were still on the air at 6:00 P.M."

"Conte Agüero's broadcasts," says Manuel Cores, who was manager of CMQ-TV, "were pro-Fidel, but they were also critical of the government. After the middle of 1959, he also became increasingly sharp in his criticism of the Communists. This caused us a lot of trouble, because the Communists now had complete control of the engineers' and announcers' unions. But the Mestre brothers, who owned the network, were determined to maintain freedom of speech no matter what happened."

During the period in which he saw Castro frequently, Conte Agüero says Fidel never discussed communism. The nearest he came to it was Fidel's attempt to describe his political philosophy as "humanism"—something between communism and democracy. Partly as a result of Conte's broadcasts, "humanism" became a popular term with the anti-Communist *Fidelistas.* Then Fidel discovered that in humanism he had created a sort of Frankinstein's monster and prohibited further use of the term. "Later," says Conte Agüero, "Aníbal Escalante, the Communist, accused me of being the inventor of 'humanism' and of poisoning Fidel's mind."

Castro began to turn cool toward Conte Agüero in the summer of 1959. "I had written a book, *Fidel Castro: His Life and Work,*" says Conte, "which was made up largely of the letters he had written to me over the years. After the first printing of 50,000 copies had been distributed on July 15, 1959, Fidel personally ordered the books recalled and destroyed. His excuse to me was that he wished to write a foreword of his own because there were certain things in the book that he didn't agree with. This puzzled me until I re-examined the book carefully. Then I understood. Most of the political ideas Fidel expressed in his early letters were those of the Ortodoxo Party which he belonged to at the time. He also had written many things that were critical of communism; and in his later letters he had reiterated his devotion to free elections, freedom of speech, the free press, etc., which he now wanted to forget. It occurred to me at that time that, if Fidel was not already flirting with communism, he certainly didn't want to do anything to offend the Communists. At any rate, my book was never republished."

When Anastas Mikoyan arrived in Cuba in February 1960, Conte Agüero was already recognized as an outspoken anti-Communist, despite his well-known friendship with Fidel Castro. Following the opening of the Soviet exhibit Conte went on the air and stated that while the Soviet exposition was worth seeing, it should convince people that the Soviet Union was far behind the U.S.A. in technological developments. This immediately drew an editorial blast from *Hoy, Revolución* and the party-line broadcasters. The campaign to destroy Conte Agüero was under way. As it raged on through February and into March, thousands of letters poured in daily to CMQ. Some of these were abusive, but there were also many from Cubans who urged Conte Agüero to keep on fighting communism. The Mestre brothers told Conte to go ahead and trade blow for blow with his adversaries.

Finally, on March 20, 1960, Conte Agüero announced over CMQ that he intended to settle the controversy once and for all in an "Open Letter to Fidel Castro." The next day the militia surrounded Radio-Centro with the idea of preventing Conte from reaching the studios of CMQ. But they had forgotten that, before going to CMQ, Conte Agüero also broadcast a half-hour radio commentary each day over Radio Progreso. When he arrived at Radio Progreso a group of friends told him what was happening at CMQ. Conte went into the studio and locked himself and the engineers inside. Then he read his letter to Fidel over the airwaves.

After the radio broadcast he made an attempt to get into Radio-Centro but found his way barred not only by the militia but by an angry, Communist-controlled mob. His only solace was the appearance of about two thousand students from Havana University, led by Alberto Muller, who put on a dramatic counter-demonstration, shouting "Down with the Communists!"

He went into hiding and heard his old friend, Fidel Castro, tear the reputation of Conte Agüero to shreds in a four-hour telecast the following week. Castro accused

Conte of being a traitor, a counter-revolutionary, a paid agent of the Yankee imperialists. He even declared that the alleged letters from Fidel Castro in the suppressed book were clever forgeries.

On the day after Conte Agüero sought asylum in the Argentine Embassy, Goar Mestre made an unscheduled personal appearance on CMQ's popular program, "Ante la Prensa," the Cuban counterpart of "Meet the Press," to reaffirm freedom of speech. The union engineers tried desperately to cut the telecast off the air, but a few loyal employees barricaded the control room. Later he slipped out of Cuba, and the CMQ-TV network, like all others in Cuba, was taken over by the unions and finally confiscated in September 1960.

# Part Four

# DISMAL SPRINGTIME

By early 1961 sabotage and guerrilla activities against the Castro regime surpassed those of the anti-Batista underground in 1958. From the Sierra Maestra in Oriente province to the Sierra de los Organos in Pinar del Río, the mountains were honeycombed with guerrilla bands that eluded and baffled Castro's combined army and militia, estimated to comprise 200,000 men. In the province of Oriente alone there were about eight hundred young freedom fighters operating under the direction of Alberto Muller of the DRE.

Every day, somewhere on the island, a major factory exploded, a government building was set afire, a railway was wrecked, a bridge destroyed. The enormous Hershey sugar mill was sabotaged; in Havana the El Encanto department store, the city's finest, went up in flames. Everywhere the night skies glowed with the reflected flames of fires that were symbolic of rising Cuban opposition to the Communist regime of Fidel Castro.

However, the anti-Castro underground also was plagued by rivalries and lack of arms and explosives with which to fight a war. Since late 1959 more than thirty different resistance groups had sprung up within Cuba; even these were splintered further when their emissaries arrived in Miami in search of arms and financial support. While this fragmentation made it difficult for Castro's intelligence services to nail down the opposition groups and leaders, such factionalism also siphoned off much of the strength and support which the movement sorely needed.

The largest group was the Movement for Revolutionary Recovery (MRR) which was eventually headed by Manuel

Artime. In June 1960 a first attempt to unite the MRR with four other groups into the Democratic Revolutionary Front was made. Another group, the People's Revolutionary Movement (MRP), was formed in the fall of 1960 headed by Manuel Ray Rivero (Manolo Ray), an engineer who had served as Castro's Minister of Public Works until November 1959 when he broke with the regime because of the imprisonment of his close friend Hubert Matos. But the MRP remained aloof from the Front until March 1961 when it joined the Cuban Revolutionary Council, a loose and uneasy coalition formed almost on the eve of the invasion.

Meanwhile, in Cuba, the active freedom fighters were paying a heavy price for the lack of coordination. Saboteurs were desperate for even the simplest forms of explosives and incendiary material. Guerrilla bands lacked arms and were forced to ration bullets and curtail firepower. "Often we would receive word through clandestine channels," says Dr. Oscar Salas, "to set signal fires at a certain location and hour and be ready for an air drop. We followed instructions to the letter. But the planes never came, or the supplies would be dropped in the wrong place and fall into the wrong hands. This happened to us more than a dozen times in Matanzas while we waited under the most hazardous conditions with militia all around us."

Nino Díaz, the rebel major who fought Castro's Communists in the Sierra Maestra, was another victim of sporadic and undependable logistics. On a moonless night in October 1960 he landed on the southeast coast of Cuba with three trusted lieutenants and headed for the Sierra which he knew so well. "Using the same old tactics," he says, "I went among the peasants and collected a force of two hundred and fifty men. But we had little more than the arms we brought with us, and what we could capture from Castro's militia. We operated in Cuba for over eighty days, then we couldn't hold out any longer. I sent out coded appeals until our radio broke down completely; but the promised supplies never came. Meanwhile, Castro's intelligence, which was working at top efficiency, had picked up our trail, and at one time they had several thousand men looking for us.

"Finally, I broke up my men into groups of five and turned them loose. One of the men in my group went foraging for food and was captured. Another stole a jeep and was caught by the militia before he could reach us. With the remaining two men I hid out for seventeen days in a poorhouse, until we could steal a small boat and get back to Florida."

### *The Fatal Rendezvous*

The military chief of the MRR within Cuba was a tall, blondish young man named Rogelio González Corzo. "Yet I don't believe there were twenty people in the underground who knew him by that name," says Cristóbal (cover name) who was his deputy. "But he was known all over Cuba, even by people who never set eyes on him, by his cover-name Francisco."

Francisco was not only a legendary character, but he was idolized by those who knew him as a young man of courage, resourcefulness and charm. He was a close friend and associate of Manuel Artime, the anti-Communist INRA deputy, who was now slated to become the commander of the military forces about to invade Cuba.

Francisco was then at loggerheads—chiefly over the issue of supplies—with another young underground leader, Rafael Díaz Hanscom. Rafael was determined to bring an end to the chaos by unifying the anti-Castro forces within Cuba. "He told me in October 1960," says Aurelio Fernandez Díaz, who was Rafael's contact in Miami, "that the exiles in Florida were wasting valuable time in squabbling over political differences instead of concentrating on the main, patriotic issue which was Cuba's freedom. So he proposed to organize the Unidad Revolucionaria [UR] which would be controlled from within Cuba. He had already signed up twenty-two groups throughout the island, and had persuaded Humberto Sorí Marín [former judge advocate of the rebel army and Castro's first Minister of Agriculture] to become the military commander."

By February 1961 the competition for supplies had become so bitter and frustrating that the whole anti-Castro cause was jeopardized. Besides, there was growing interest in Rafael's UR since the success of any invasion of the island would depend largely on well-coordinated uprisings and sabotage activities. Says Andrés Zayas, known as "Justo" in the underground: "With this in mind, I brought Francisco and Rafael together in a friend's house. They agreed to work together, and we then planned a full-scale meeting at which Sorí Marín and other key underground leaders would be present."

The important, and fateful, meeting was scheduled for 6:30 P.M., Saturday, March 18. "That day Francisco came to my home in the Miramar section of Havana for luncheon," says Cristóbal. "The meeting had been planned with the utmost care. Neither Francisco nor any of the other participants knew exactly where it would take place. According to our system, certain trusted couriers, each unknown to the others, would come at an agreed-upon time and escort each individual to the secret meeting-place. As we sat at luncheon, Francisco was preoccupied with plans for operations in Pinar del Río province, which was to be his territory. At one point, he knocked over a glass of water and never seemed to notice. But he made one statement which later haunted me.

" 'How awful it would be,' he said, 'if they caught me

right here in Havana before I can even get things going in Pinar del Río.' "

Shortly before 5:00 P.M., "Justo" Zayas, who was supposed to attend the meeting, came by Cristóbal's home to report that an arms shipment was due that evening. "You won't need me at the meeting," he told Francisco, "particularly with Sorí Marín there." "No," Francisco answered, "we can get along without you. It's more important for you to pick up the 'toys.' "

At 5:45, Cristina Nogueira, an underground courier, came to Cristóbal's home to escort Francisco to the meeting. "We got into the car," she says, "and I drove over a carefully specified route to the designated house. When we entered the apartment, a man and a woman, both of whom belonged to my group, were seated in the front room playing canasta. They merely nodded and I escorted Francisco to a room in the rear. Rafael, Sorí Marín and a number of others were already there. He went into the meeting and I sat down with the canasta players."

Shortly after 6:10 there was a light tap on the front door and one of the canasta players went and opened it cautiously. Armed militiamen swarmed into the apartment. Cristina ran to a window and saw the army trucks in the street and the house completely surrounded by armed men. Francisco, Rafael and the other underground leaders were captured. Sorí Marín drew a pistol and tried to shoot his way out. He was badly wounded.

With one swoop, Castro's intelligence people had corralled the key figures in the "unified revolutionary underground." The freedom movement never recovered from the blow.

Ana María (cover name), Cristóbal's fiancée, was the courier who delivered Humberto Sorí Marín to the fateful meeting. She arrived before Cristina and Francisco, but declined to join the canasta players because she had another assignment to complete.

"When I returned about an hour later," she says, "I saw the trucks and the swarm of militiamen from a block away, and I managed to swerve the car into a narrow alley and into the next street. Then I drove madly to the place where I knew Cristóbal was holding a meeting."

Cristóbal was shocked and sobered by the news. "Francisco's capture was a catastrophe," he says, "but in addition to that I had the sickening realization that I had been delegated to take over his duties if anything happened to him, and I knew I could never fill Francisco's shoes. But then I had a glimmer of hope. Perhaps Francisco had eluded the captors. [The details of the raid were still unknown to Cristóbal.] You had to remember that he was a very brave and resourceful fellow. So I immediately put in a call for Margarita Rosa, who was Francisco's confidential aide, and asked her to meet me at a certain place."

That night Cristóbal and Margarita Rosa cautiously reconnoitered the environs of the raided meeting place. "There was just a bare chance that Francisco might have escaped," she says, "because there were narrow alleys on both sides of the house and a vacant lot behind it. But I had a strong feeling that he hadn't made it. There was only one other hope: the odds were about a thousand to one that Castro's G-2 didn't realize that the man they had was Rogelio González Corzo—the much-wanted Francisco. Few people knew him by sight; he had dyed his blond hair and eyebrows black and his whole appearance had been altered since any photograph had been taken.

"After I left Cristóbal that night, I put in a telephone call to my contact in Miami. She was presumably just a girl friend, and I was supposed to have a boy friend in Miami. 'This is Margarita Rosa,' I said brightly. 'Please tell my friend that I am coming over to spend a few days with you and will expect to see much of him.'

"My 'friend' was Dr. Manuel Artime, who was now chief of the Liberation Army. I knew that he would sense that something was terribly wrong when he got the message. I had previously made eight trips between Havana and Miami as Francisco's courier. When I left Miami the last time, less than a month before, Artime had given me firm orders that I must not attempt it again. So, now he would know. . . ."

### *Deep Infiltration*

On Monday morning, March 20, the attractive fashionably dressed young woman who was known only to the underground as Margarita Rosa, boarded a plane bound for Miami. She carried a Cuban passport made out in her maiden name and stating her occupation as "housewife," although she actually was a social worker, the wife of a Havana physician, and the mother of three small children. Yet she encountered none of the red tape which harassed the other Cubans who were to be her fellow passengers. Indeed, she seemed to be on friendly and even intimate terms with the immigration and G-2 personnel at the airport.

"Actually, in those days, many Cubans traveled back and forth quite freely between Havana and Miami," she says, "and I'm certain that many were Castro agents. Perhaps the fact that I did return to Cuba from each trip made things easier. However, I knew that the G-2 wasn't easily fooled, and I was aware that I was taking a big chance. I could only hope that they considered me a rich, somewhat flighty young woman who was having an affair in Florida."

In Miami, Margarita Rosa immediately called Artime and he named a rendezvous. When they met he seemed greatly disturbed. She told him about the raided meeting on the preceding Saturday, and that they had to assume that Francisco had been captured.

"But I also told him about a plan I had discussed with Cristóbal. We had our own contacts inside Castro's G-2, and I was rather certain that for a sum like $50,000 we might be able to buy Francisco's release or arrange for his escape. Artime considered the scheme ridiculous; but when I insisted and told him we could raise the money in Havana, he agreed that we might try it.

"Artime obviously had other things to worry about. When I asked cautiously about the invasion plans, he only shook his head and said that 'many things have been changed.' I told him that Cristóbal and the others were prepared to carry out Francisco's plan. The basis of those plans was that internal uprisings must be coordinated with the landings, and that extensive sabotage had to be staged to disrupt Castro's defenses or counter-offensive. For this, I said, we needed a date or, at least, adequate warning in advance. Artime said that this would have to come from 'our American friends.'"

Margarita Rosa returned to Havana and got her "ransom" plan under way. She personally raised the $50,000 (in pesos). Contact was established with the people in G-2. Arrangements were even made for asylum in an embassy for Francisco and for Margarita Rosa and her family. Success seemed so certain that she placed two bottles of champagne in her refrigerator to be opened on the night of the "delivery."

"We occupied a two-floor apartment," she explains. "My physician-husband used the first floor for his offices and examining rooms, and the upper floor served as living quarters for ourselves and three children. One afternoon early in April, I was working in an office looking out upon my husband's waiting-room. This, as usual, was filled with patients. I was vaguely aware of *two* male patients entering the doctor's office. Then I noticed a stranger, seated in the waiting room, watching me closely.

"I went to my husband's office and tapped on the door, and as I did so the stranger followed me. I opened the door and saw my husband seated at his desk. Standing over him was a man holding a gun, and another man was searching through the files. 'Come in,' my husband said. 'These are some friends from G-2. They have already found your purse which contains a lot of money.' "

Margarita Rosa and her husband were taken first to the G-2 headquarters (a converted mansion on Havana's Fifth Avenue); after preliminary questioning she was sent to a prison in Pinar del Río. There she met the underground courier, Cristina Nogueira, who told her the details of the raid and Francisco's capture.

The interrogations of Margarita Rosa at G-2 headquarters and later in prison, caused her to believe that the only real evidence against her was the handbag containing the $50,000, plus a cigarette lighter, picked up in her apartment, which unfortunately bore the embossed seal of the MRR! She felt confident that she, like probably thousands of other Cubans at the moment, was suspected only of being a 'counter-revolutionary' and a possible accomplice of the CIA. But then she was turned over to a Captain Antonio Valenzuela, who was an entirely different type of interrogator.

"He was a taller-than-average man, about fifty years old, with a dark mustache and dark hair flecked with gray," she says. "He seemed gentle in comparison to the others, smooth but crafty. As I learned later, he was as much a brainwasher and political indoctrinator as he was a G-2 interrogator."

Valenzuela's first remark stunned the girl. "Well, how does it feel to be in prison, *Margarita Rosa?*" he asked.

"Before I could say anything," she says, "he told me: 'Margarita Rosa, we know that you are the only woman on the MRR national staff. Francisco is your boss. Now, let me draw you a diagram.' He took a pencil and paper and drew an absolutely accurate diagram of our organization from top to bottom. Then he said: 'I will now read you a very interesting schedule.' He opened a folder and began to read dates, hours, places, names—a complete record of my trips to and from Miami, my meetings with Artime and other people, everything that I had done with my time. They knew everything, and they had known all along!"

Thus she was faced with the shocking truth which many Cubans soon realized to their dismay. Castro's intelligence and counter-intelligence services, thanks probably to their Soviet mentors, had penetrated into nearly every pocket and corner of the underground movement.

### *"Army of Liberation"*

Meanwhile, in Florida, hundreds of young Cubans had been enlisting enthusiastically in what became known later as the Army of Liberation. As originally conceived early in 1960, with the blessing and support of the U.S. government, it was to be a small force of about 500 tough, highly trained, well-armed guerrillas who would infiltrate Cuba in small groups and landing parties and then link up with the local freedom fighters of the underground. These underground forces also were to be supplied with arms and explosives for sabotage and guerrilla activities.

The men of the Liberation Army were recruited principally in Miami and, after careful screening, they were sent to isolated camps in the swamps of Florida and Louisiana for basic training. Later, they were shipped to tactical training centers in the mountains of Guatemala and finally to bases in Nicaragua which would serve as staging areas for the assaults on the home island. Obsolete

World War II B-26s and C-47s, flown by competent Cuban pilots and crews, provided a small but adequate air arm.

"Our number never exceeded fifteen hundred men," says one veteran officer. "This sounds pitifully small, but our two greatest assets were morale and fighting spirit. We were convinced that we would succeed, despite Castro's vastly larger forces which, we knew, were equipped with Soviet arms. We still are convinced that we would have triumphed—if the operations had been carried out as originally planned. But, of course, they were not. The plans were constantly being changed, until the original objectives were lost. Instead of infiltrating, making multiple landings, we wound up by making a one-shot invasion, and even that without preliminary naval or aerial bombardment, without air cover and support, and without the coordinated operations of the underground. The freedom fighters in Cuba were taken completely by surprise."

## *D-Day Minus Two*

At dawn on Saturday, April 15, twenty-six-year-old Salvador Miralles, a grinning, pint-size cocky Cuban known as the "Evil Midget," sat in the left-hand seat of an ancient two-engine Martin B-26 bomber perched for take-off on a hidden airfield near Puerto Cabezas on the coast of Nicaragua. His jerky gestures betrayed his impatience as the co-pilot ran through the last checklist items; then his small feet pressed firmly on the brakes as engine No. 1 and then engine No. 2 coughed and roared into action and quickly ran up to takeoff speed.

Miralles released the brakes and the plane roared down the runway, climbed, and turned on to the designated heading; only then did Miralles relax and give the thumbs-up signal to his co-pilot. This was it! At long last, they were going to bomb Havana and the San Antonio de los Baños airfield, the base of Castro's puny "air force."

Miralles already had flown two missions over Cuba. On the first he had dropped nothing more lethal than propaganda leaflets—in which he managed to conceal a few rocks. The second was an arms drop over the Escambray Mountains; the confusion of ground signals led him within range of anti-aircraft fire which knocked out his radio and one engine. Both missions he considered humiliating experiences which he felt compelled to avenge on this first flight with full bomb load.

Just at dawn three B-26s (with the Evil Midget in the lead) approached the San Antonio de los Baños field on the outskirts of Havana and lined up for the bomb run.

"I couldn't swear how much damage we did to Castro's aircraft," Miralles says, "but the field looked almost like a miniature Pearl Harbor. After dropping the bombs we made eight or nine passes at the field using our machine guns at about 1,200 feet before the anti-aircraft fire got too thick." The three planes in the Miralles' element made the home base in Nicaragua safely and with little damage.

The Evil Midget and his comrades were keyed up by this first taste of combat. Then came the word that the second mission, scheduled for Sunday, April 16, had been cancelled. "Higher headquarters" wanted to sit tight for forty-eight hours to "estimate public reaction." Says Miralles: "That drew a tremendous howl of protest. What did 'public reaction' have to do with it? The men were very depressed until, on Sunday afternoon, we got word that the next mission would be the Bahía de Cochinos [Bay of Pigs], where the invasion was scheduled to take place the next morning, April 17.

"Then we were angry and bewildered. 'Why did we bomb on Saturday?' the men asked. 'Were we messenger boys sent to warn Castro in advance to get things ready for the big show?' "

## *Patriots in the Dark*

The consternation of the pilots was mild compared to that which prevailed from Havana to Oriente immediately after the bombs were dropped on Saturday morning, April 15. Everyone was certain that the raid was a prelude to the long-expected invasion. But the maddening questions were: When? Where? Are we free to move? No one in the underground knew the answers. The only person who seemed to be acting with firmness and direction was Fidel Castro.

Cristóbal listened with dismay to Castro's statement broadcast over Radio Centro on Saturday morning: "All commands have been put on a state of alert. If this air attack should be the prelude to an invasion, the country will resist and will destroy with a mailed fist any force which disembarks on our soil. . . ."

Cristóbal and "Justo" Zayas, who had taken over the command posts in the underground vacated by Francisco and Rafael, were besieged by frantic appeals for instructions. "All we could do," says Cristóbal, "was to repeat the standing order: 'Do *nothing* until you receive instructions.' This was even more maddening to us than to the men in the field. Despite setbacks, the underground was still in fair shape. I am positive that, given the word, we could have carried out the major plan of coordinated uprisings and sabotage. But we were told nothing. We were left completely in the dark. We really knew less than Fidel Castro."

Later Castro stated: "We knew that the air raid [of April 15th] was not just a harassment, but a military operation designed to destroy our air force. Therefore we figured the aggression would come soon. . . . Tactically speaking [the air raid] was an error because it gave us a chance to take measures. We mobilized all combat units."

Throughout Saturday and Sunday, Darío Prados, a

stout, palefaced youth of twenty-four who had been trained as a radio operator in Guatemala and slipped into Cuba late in March, hunched over his black boxes futilely endeavoring to establish contact with headquarters outside Cuba. He got no response. Cristóbal insisted that he keep trying. So, for several hours, Prados tapped out his coded call, waited for an answer, then rechecked his equipment, and tapped again and again.

Between calls, while checking his receiver, he picked up a message broadcast at 6.5 megacycles which only increased his and Cristóbal's bewilderment. It was repeated several times in Spanish and English: "Alert, alert. . . . Look well at the rainbow. . . . The fish will rise very soon. . . . Chico is in the house. . . . Visit him. . . . The sky is blue. . . . Place notice in the tree. . . . The tree is green and brown. . . . The letters arrived well. . . . The letters are white. . . . The fish will not take much time to rise. . . . The fish is red. . . . Look well at the rainbow. . . ."

Says Cristóbal: "Surely that meant *something,* but if it was meant for us, then somebody had forgotten to give us the code! I still don't know what it was all about."

Late on Sunday, Darío Prados let out a startled cry for Cristóbal's attention. He had established contact. "But the brief exchange was far from satisfying," says Cristóbal. "We were told that the operation would take place shortly; we were to keep in contact but *do nothing*—repeat *nothing*—until we received orders."

Prados, wearing the uniform of a Castro militiaman, which might make things easier in case he had to flee, maintained radio contact through the early hours of April 17, listening for the orders which never came. To keep awake he tried to analyze the strange "luck"—good and bad—that had dogged him ever since he landed in Cuba with his load of waterproof black boxes.

The underground contact had picked him up in a stolen

jeep with INRA markings. "This got us safely into Havana," he says. "We even had a flat tire, which some passing militiamen helped us change. But while we stood chatting on the roadside I almost choked on the cigarette I was smoking. It was a popular U.S. brand now unobtainable in Cuba! I ground the butt under my heel, hoping the militia boys wouldn't sense the distinctive odor of the smoke."

Prado's luck lasted. Three men in the five-man team that had come ashore were picked up by Castro's G-2, and the fourth simply vanished. Prados was the only one left. But, on April 18, Prados narrowly escaped capture when his underground hideaway in the suburbs of Havana was raided by G-2. The lieutenant in command of the raiding party was the "missing" man. Prados recalls bitterly, "That guy attended our meetings in Miami, he had gone through training with us in Guatemala, and had been last one ashore when we 'infiltrated' Cuba!"

Several minutes before 4:00 A.M. on Monday, April 17, César Prieto, then a sergeant in the Revolutionary Army, was on duty in the guard room of the new Gramma Base near Quiebra Hacha in Pinar del Río when the intercom crackled and a voice announced: "Attention, attention. Stand by for further orders to fight enemy aggression at the Bahía de Cochinos. . . . Stand by. . . ."

A few hours later, Sergeant Prieto, riding in a Soviet jeep at the head of a battalion of trucks mounted with anti-aircraft guns, pulled into the Central Australia, a sugar mill 25 kilometers from the beachhead, where Fidel Castro had set up headquarters. "This was a beautiful morning," Prieto recalls, "and the 334-kilometer trip was peaceful and uneventful, almost like maneuvers. The roads were jammed with mobile equipment; our convoy from Gramma Base alone consisted of sixty trucks. I kept scanning the skies for enemy aircraft but saw nothing."

Like Prieto's outfit, units of Castro's army and militia converged on Las Villas province from all parts of Cuba and virtually without opposition. Alfonso Rodríguez, an underground leader in Cárdenas, 100 miles east of Havana, had sat up all night with his wife, Carmen, listening for the word. At 5:15 A.M., they heard the "freedom station" on Swan Island off the Honduras coast announce: "This is the day. . . . An Army of Liberation is in Cuba to fight with you against the Communist tyranny of the unbalanced Fidel Castro. . . ."

"Good God, they've started without us!" Rodríguez cried, close to tears. "What can we do?" Level-headed Carmen Rodríguez gave a woman's answer: "Dress and leave this house immediately. You'll be among the first the G-2 will come looking for. I'll take the children to my mother's. Now hurry!" Alfonso Rodríguez went to a hiding place; but on the way he saw the truckloads of troops moving eastward, and he thought bitterly of the precious cache of C-3 plastic explosives with which his cell had planned to knock out the bridges at this critical moment.

In a small café on the outskirts of Santiago, the Rev. Humberto Muñiz, a handsome, thirty-six-year-old Protestant minister who had laid aside his cloth to lead the fight against Castro and communism, sat with four lieutenants awaiting the word which would set in motion a plan that would bottle up Castro's mobile units stationed near the eastern end of the island. "Padre Humberto" had assured his men that the orders surely would come. Instead, at 4:00 P.M., the music blaring from the radio ceased suddenly and they heard the official government announcement that "troops landed by air and sea are attacking national territory south of Las Villas. . . ." The four men stared incredulously at Humberto, as he got up and left the place in a daze.

"Dear Lord," he prayed, "what have I done wrong?

Where did I fail? Whom did I forget to contact? Why are my people left impotent at this hour?" Not until many hours after the disaster was Padre Humberto able to convince himself that the failure was not his. He was only one of many brave, resourceful but forgotten freedom fighters who, on that black Monday, had to learn about the invasion of Cuba only after the fantastic blunder had been made.

### *Embarrassing Questions*

The Bay of Pigs tragedy probably will haunt some men for the rest of their days; but the bitterest memories will abide longest in the minds of Cubans who tried valiantly and failed, and were cruelly frustrated.

Nino Díaz, in command of 158 trained guerrillas, was aboard a derelict cargo ship on Sunday, April 16, with orders to make a diversionary landing at the mouth of the Río Mocambo between Baracoa and Guantánamo. Late that night he sent ashore a reconnoitering party in a small boat which ran into an ambush. "The beach was alive with troops," he says. "There was a twisting line of blinking lights that puzzled me; these proved to be the tail-lights of the army trucks coming from Guantánamo City blinking on and off as they used brakes." He radioed Guatemala for instructions. "We were jubilant when orders came for us to join the main invasion force landing on Playa Girón in the Bahía de Cochinos."

Many hours later, after the invasion forces landed, Nino approached the Las Villas coast and sighted several troopships—pulling *away* from the beachhead! "Because our old banana boat was flying the Costa Rican flag and we were wearing Castro-style uniforms," he says, "the ships thought we were an enemy decoy and opened fire. I managed to make contact with a walkie-talkie, identified ourselves, and asked permission to join the landing. The captain replied that they weren't going to land—Castro's Soviet guns and tanks controlled the beach, all was lost.

"The ships pulled away. Our old boat was in bad shape and couldn't make more than eight knots. Guatemala warned me by radio to stay away from Florida. We finally made Vieques Island off Puerto Rico."

Sergeant César Prieto was with the Castro anti-aircraft battalion eight kilometers north of Playa Girón on Tuesday morning, April 18. "We expected the U.S. planes to attack at dawn," he says. "But only one B-26 came over. We shot it down, of course; and why not? We had thirty-six anti-aircraft guns trained on that lone plane. The slaughter made me feel ashamed."

Salvador Miralles, the Evil Midget, still flying his B-26, made a last sortie over Cuba that morning with better luck. "Castro had only six planes in the air that day," he says, "but the jets were too much for us. I saw a British-made Sea Fury trail one of our C-47s, which had just dropped paratroops, and shoot it down in flames. Just as I was pulling out, I saw a convoy of Castro's anti-aircraft trucks heading for the beach. I had nothing left but my machine guns but I opened the throttle and strafed that column with everything I had.

"I didn't have enough gas left to make Nicaragua, so I headed for Florida. About ten miles off the Cuban coast I saw an American aircraft carrier [USS *Boxer*] with an escort of ten destroyers and all her planes on deck. I could not resist yelling out loud: 'Damn you, Yankees, come on! They're slaughtering us.' I felt rather foolish, but I broke down and cried."

Bernardo Ramos, operations officer at the Nicaraguan field, flew three missions in a C-47. Twice he dropped paratroopers. The third mission was to land and pick up wounded on the beachhead. "There were no wounded," he says. "It was all over. That was Thursday morning. When we got back to Puerto Cabezas the base was in mourning. We had one American, a civilian named Simpson, and I heard him raising hell with headquarters. He was the one who had promised that we would have air cover, and now he was swearing at someone about the American breach of faith. They must have recalled him, because he took off that morning and we never saw him again."

Today there are scores of articulate Cubans, veterans of the Bahía de Cochinos fiasco, who suddenly go dumb and merely shrug or scowl when the dubious role of the United States in the operation is mentioned. The most one can get out of them usually comes in pointed, painful, embarrassing questions: Why wasn't the Cuban underground alerted until it was too late? Why was the promised air cover of the beachhead called off? Finally, who gave the green light for the invasion—and why—knowing that the plan had been emasculated and that the operation was doomed to failure? The relatively few Cubans who ask such questions add pointedly: "The answers can come only from the United States."

### *Castro Cracks Down*

Perhaps a handful of Cubans heard the weak voice of the clandestine radio broadcasting from the Sierra Escambray on the morning of April 20: "Many of our troops managed to flee to the Escambray Mountains to continue the attack. We do not expect to overthrow Castro immediately or without setbacks. We were not expecting to face Soviet arms directed by Communist advisors and emerge unscathed."

The plaintive voice was drowned out by the Havana radio trumpeting to Cuba—and all Latin America—that "the revolution has been victorious. . . . Cubans are now exterminating the invaders. . . . Yankee imperialism has suffered another glaring defeat. . . . The myth of Yankee invincibility has been destroyed by Fidel Castro. . . . Leaders of Yankee imperialism should learn their lesson, or one day the world will learn that the United States has been reduced to ashes."

Castro's triumphant broadcasts blared loudest in the prisons, jails and improvised internment centers which now swarmed with hapless Cubans whom the secret police and neighborhood informers had marked as counter-revolutionaries, traitors and plain *gusanos* (worms). The roundups started on the eve of the invasion, April 16; by Thursday (April 20) the already crowded prisons such as La Cabaña and El Príncipe were jammed. Police stations and G-2 centers were overflowing with bewildered men and women. Schools, theaters, sports arenas were used as jails and soon became foul-smelling, disease-breeding hellholes.

The earliest crackdown crippled the underground. "Justo" Zayas lost fourteen top men in the first sweep of the dragnet, guided by G-2 infiltrators, and barely escaped capture himself. Cristóbal and a few of his men switched hideouts from house to house, usually a few steps ahead of G-2 agents. "No one could be trusted," he says. "Terrorized people were turning in any stranger they saw. Our men were being picked up one by one. We finally lost contact; it was a case of survival, every man for himself."

Vicente Rubiera Feíto, the deposed union leader, but still an employee of the nationalized telephone company, was at work in the Havana exchange on Monday morning, April 17, when the doors of the building were locked and no one was permitted to leave. "They rounded up all employees," he says, "and called off the names of those who had any record of anti-Communist activities. About a hundred of us were loaded into trucks and taken to Morro Castle. Over 5,000 people were detained there, more than the place could hold. The women were sent inside the old fortress, the men were left outside in the high-walled yards. We were there for two days in the cold rain without food or covering, then they sorted us out and sent us to other prisons."

A roundup of Catholic priests, including the hierarchy, began on Monday (April 17) with the broadcast announcement that "G-2 agents have arrested Eduardo Boza Masvidal [Auxiliary Archbishop of Havana] and [Father] Arnelio Blanco Blanco, cassocked thugs, in La Caridad church in Reina Street." Father Diego Madrigal was arrested by militiamen as he came from the altar after saying 10 o'clock Mass and was taken to the G-2 prison. "I found myself in a small cell, barely big enough for three persons, with nine other priests and ten laymen. We were there for 18 days, without sanitary facilities or food, standing all the time, except when one was taken out for interrogation, abuse, and unmentionable indignities."

### *The Dragnet*

In Havana alone 20,000 persons were arrested between April 15 and April 20, Mercedes Morejón, a thirty-five-year-old bank secretary, was picked up by militiamen on the street, for no apparent reason, and taken to the Havana Sports Palace (Ciudad Deportiva). "We were forced to squat on the floor between the seats in the huge circular arena," she says. "Militiamen occupied the seats at intervals and threatened to shoot if we raised our heads or stood up. The place was jammed with several thousand people of all descriptions. I remember them bringing in a man with a fractured leg in a cast, and a chef from the Hilton Hotel who arrived wearing his tall white cap. Near me on the floor was a Negro woman from Jamaica who was arrested at a bus stop merely because the militiamen overheard her speaking English. After nearly twenty-four hours I was transferred to Príncipe Prison where women never had been incarcerated before. The overcrowding, sickness and filth there were indescribable."

Ernesto Santamarina was arrested in his Havana home and taken to the huge Blanquita movie theater, once billed as the world's largest. "The house seats 4,000, I believe," he says, "but this time it was a case of standing room only. The noise, tension, hysteria were beyond belief. The lieutenant in charge made things worse with his constant haranguing from the stage. He said we *gusanos* were going to be kept there until the last traitor and counter-revolutionary was identified and shot. The noise and tension unnerved some of the young, trigger-happy militiamen, and several bursts were fired from machine guns. Many people were wounded, and three young men were killed.

Dr. Mario Seigle, one of the captured physicians in the Blanquita, helped set up an improvised dispensary on the balcony. "There wasn't much we could do," he says, "except give the simplest kind of first aid. We had no drugs, instruments, bandages, and we needed everything including sedatives for hysterical women. We had several births and at least one serious miscarriage.

"The Blanquita was designed for air-conditioning which, of course, wasn't functioning. The stench in the unventilated auditorium was overpowering. The men's room had only three toilets, three urinals, and a janitor's washtub. This, like the ladies' room, was used by both sexes, and the line seemed endless. The drinking fountains were out of order, and people drank the water from the washtub, without cups, using their unclean hands.

"Then I discovered that the floor in the men's room had cracked, and the filthy water covering it was seeping through. That was when the gastro-intestinal disorders swept through the place, making it even more of a nightmare. But I was more fearful of typhoid and other epidemic diseases. We had taken up a collection and persuaded the militiamen to go out and buy some basic drugs. But now I took my life in my hands and began yelling for the public health people. We were in the Blanquita almost a week before they responded; but when they came and saw the conditions they agreed with me that the government might have a serious epidemic on its hands which could spread through the city. By that time, however, in addition to all our other troubles, we had thirteen people go stark, raving mad, and one elderly woman who tried to commit suicide by slashing her throat and wrists with a broken bottle."

The conditions were duplicated all over Cuba. In Matanzas, 8,000 men and women were imprisoned in a large poultry cooperative, about one hundred persons to each chicken house, swarming with insects, without hygienic facilities, sleeping on the filthy floors.

Margarita Rosa heard the stories of these widespread inhumanities from new arrivals at the prison in Pinar del Río where she was still undergoing the patient "brainwashing" by Captain Valenzuela who, for reasons of his own, was determined to "salvage" this remarkable young woman for the revolution. But there was also one bit of news which her captors broadcast freely to the assembled prisoners. These were the lists of "traitors and counterrevolutionaries" executed each day by the firing squads. On April 20 Margarita Rosa was startled to hear, on the list of those executed that morning, the names of Rafael Díaz, Humberto Sorí Marín and others who had been caught at the fateful "unification" meeting. She held her breath as other names were called. At the very end, she heard it: "Harold Boves del Castillo."

"That was Francisco," she says. "He carried a driver's license made out in the name of Harold Boves del Castillo. Even then, I was convinced, they still didn't realize that they had killed Francisco. But he, Rogelio González Corzo, died a martyr's death in La Cabaña on April 20, 1961."

Her head was still unbowed, her spirit unbroken, and her mind was her own. She spoke bluntly to Valenzuela about the mass arrests and incarcerations. "What do you expect to gain by such mass brutality?" she asked. Captain Valenzuela answered firmly: "We are determined to separate the counter-revolutionaries from the *gusanos* and exterminate them forever. We will also break the spirit of the *gusanos*, if they have any, and teach them by terror that nothing like the Bahía de Cochinos must ever happen again."

"Then allow me to tell you what you really are accomplishing," said Margarita Rosa. "You are inflaming the people with anger, making their souls cry out against such outrages. You are instilling a wonderful new spirit in the 'worms' and, I assure you, some day these 'worms' will destroy 'The Horse' [Fidel Castro] as well as all the 'Horseflies' swarming around him."

# Part Five

# DARKNESS DESCENDS

The Communist assault on Cuban education began early in 1959. The first target, significantly, was Fidel Castro's alma mater, the two-hundred-year-old University of Havana, national center of culture and a traditional stronghold of Cuban freedom.

University autonomy—complete self-government and freedom from state interference—was a jealously guarded tradition, officially conceded in 1933 and guaranteed in the Constitution of 1940. Behind this safeguard operated the Federation of University Students (FEU) which always was fiercely anti-authoritarian. Twice during the Batista dictatorship, in 1935–1936 and 1956–1959, the university was forced to close down because of the revolutionary activities of the FEU, yet Batista's all-powerful political police never dared to set foot upon the university grounds.

Fidel Castro knew well, both as a former student and as an emerging dictator, the power and the danger of the university as a political force. The real reason why he had delayed his triumphant entry into Havana until January 8, 1959, was that the FEU contingent in the rebel army, which harbored suspicions of Castro's political intentions, had seized the presidential palace and surrendered only after a deal was made for their participation in the government by President Urrutia. Said one student leader: "We fear that Fidel, because of this enormous wave of enthusiasm, will try to create an impregnable and unopposed position for himself, and this will not be good for Cuba. If he does this he will become a military dictator, and we did not fight for this."

The Castro regime gave top priority to a triple objective: do away with university autonomy; infiltrate and control the FEU; reform the university along Marxist-Leninist lines.

The University Council, the autonomous governing body made up of the deans of the thirteen faculties or schools and the eighty-two-year-old rector of the University, Dr. Clemente Inclán Costa, meanwhile set up a Mixed Commission for University Reform whose main assignment was to purge the faculties of professors and instructors linked to the Batista regime. Election of officers of the FEU were scheduled for October 1959.

Despite the purges of the pro-Batista professors, the Communists were unsatisfied. In February, they held a rally on the campus and named a new "Revolutionary Dean" of the medical school who in turn installed a new board of the University Hospital. "The majority of the Faculty of Medicine fought back vigorously," says Dr. J. M. Portuondo. "This was reported in the still-free press, and became the first public denunciation of Communist tactics. The same thing was tried in the other faculties. But the student body staunchly supported the university administration, and the Communists backed down—temporarily. They realized that they could accomplish nothing, except quiet infiltration, until they gained control of the FEU."

By September 1959 the shuffling of candidates for president of the FEU, who was to be elected by popular vote of the university's 22,000 students, resulted in the emergence of Pedro Luis Boitel, an engineering student, who appeared to be the odds-on favorite. But then a surprise candidate popped up—Major Rolando Cubela, who had been military attaché of the Cuban Embassy in Madrid during the early months of the Castro regime and later returned to become an undersecretary in Castro's Ministry of Government.

Major Cubela had been in his final year of medical school when the university closed down in 1956; since the reopening he had passed his final examinations in all subjects but one—pediatrics. Hence, he was still technically a student in September 1959 when he resigned his government post and returned to the University as a candidate for the presidency of the FEU.

The candidates and student leaders, including Boitel and Cubela, were summoned to a meeting in the office of Raúl Castro, at which Dr. Armando Hart Dávalos, Minister of Education, Carlos Franqui, editor of *Revolución,* and other government officers were present. There Raúl Castro announced that "for the good of the revolution" a single slate, headed by Major Cubela, should be entered in the university elections. The student leaders indignantly refused; those who had been backing other candidates now joined forces to support Boitel.

News of official interference made the student body seethe with resentment, and a hot pre-election campaign (Boitel *vs* Cubela) got under way. Fidel Castro made a personal appeal to Boitel to withdraw in the interest of "unity." Then, on the morning of the election, *Revolución* appeared with a front-page editorial, signed by Castro, which denounced "certain confused leaders" who had raised the "question of autonomy, as if it were possible in the midst of this revolutionary process to separate the concepts of the university, the government and the people." He called upon the students to "give each other a revolutionary embrace, *unanimously proclaim a president,* and unite in a true reform plan which will be carried out without further delay."

That morning, after the voting was under way, Major Cubela arrived on the campus in an open convertible—accompanied by Raúl Castro. Then Armando Hart and others appeared to demonstrate the government's support of Cubela and, privately, to urge Boitel to make a last-minute withdrawal.

"The pressure on Boitel was unbearable," says Luis Boza Domínguez, a leader of the anti-Castro students. "So he called a general assembly of students in the university's Plaza Cadenas and offered to resign his candidacy. It was then that the students wrote a glorious page in the university's long history of representative democracy. They refused to let Boitel resign and demanded that the voting continue. For the first time a demand of Fidel Castro had been refused."

In the end, however, the carefully planned Communist strategy prevailed. After the appearance of Castro's *Revolución* diatribe, many students decided that Boitel was doomed, and went home. Later in the day the Havana radio broadcast a false report that "Boitel has withdrawn in deference to unity." More disappointed students left the campus. Less than fifty per cent of the 22,000 students cast their ballots. The Castro candidate, Major Cubela, was elected president of the FEU by a slim margin. (Later, Pedro Luis Boitel was arrested as a counter-revolutionary and sentenced, without trial, to thirty years imprisonment.)

### *Death of a University*

The technique which the Communists employed so successfully in the labor unions and elsewhere now was applied to the university. After the contrived election came the purge of students and faculty members, the revision of the curriculum, and the installation of a Communist faculty.

The first step came soon after Cubela's election with the formation of the student militia. "Again the regime collided with the students' resistance," says Dr. Andrés Valdespino, a professor of law. "Out of 22,000 students, less than three hundred signed up for the militia. But this noisy minority compensated for its smallness with blatant exhibitionism. Day and night they tramped through the academic halls carrying pistols, rifles, and machine guns. The university became a barracks."

Says Francisco García, then an engineering student: "There were militiamen in every classroom, and their duty was to observe and report to the G-2 those of us who were anti-Castro."

The persecution and expulsion of anti-Communist students began in the early spring of 1960, following the demonstration against Mikoyan and the defense of commentator Luis Conte Agüero (see pp. 91–96). First, Major Cubela and his cohorts tried to set up "Disciplinary Tribunals" but quickly dropped the idea when they learned that, until the government enacted a new education law, the accused students would have the right to defend themselves and thus stir up campus support. The alternative was direct action—violence.

"Incidents" were created: on the night of May 5, for example, a burlap bag loaded with cartridges was placed upon the doorstep of the FEU and ignited. When the cartridges exploded, Major Cubela howled that the "counter-revolutionary" students were attacking the FEU. He hastily convened a general assembly to which he was careful to invite—by telegraph—left-wing delegations from Havana secondary schools, labor unions, and other non-university groups.

"On May 7," says Luis Boza Domínguez, "the campus was overflowing with Communist thugs, militiamen out of uniform, and strong-arm men provided by the labor unions. Cubela whipped the mob into a frenzy: 'These miserable beings, these traitors who dare to accuse the FEU of treason! They are the aggressors, the provocateurs. They should be in the military prisons with the war criminals where they can be tried by the revolutionary tribunals. But since we have no disciplinary tribunals these things must be handled by the students themselves. Because we cannot allow these miserable beings to continue coming to the university in order to upset the revolution."

The mob responded with the cries of "*Paredón! Paredón!*" The militiamen, posted at strategic places, kept all non-Communist students away from the demonstration. However, a lone engineering student, Joaquin Pérez, managed to get by, was recognized, seized and brutally beaten. The Communist press and radio took up the cry next day and Communist-inspired protests poured in upon the authorities demanding the expulsion of the "traitors." Says Boza Domínguez: "Those who were not expelled were driven out by violence and intimidation. There was nothing left but to join Alberto Muller and the others in the underground. Rolando Cubela unwittingly had become a first-class recruiting officer for the anti-Castro Directorate of Revolutionary Students (DRE)."

The final assault on university autonomy began in June with another contrived incident. "Several Communist students in the Engineering School," says Dr. J. M. Portuondo, "demanded that the examinations be held without the presence of proctors and in a certain room which provided no safeguards against cheating. The faculty rejected the demands, and the students declared that this was an affront to their honor.

"The professors involved were summarily 'fired' by the students' association and replaced with professors of the students' own choice.

"The University Council denounced this action and immediately drew fire from Cubela's FEU in the form of a 'manifesto' which maligned not only the council but most of the faculty. Groups of revolutionary students began taking charge of the schools and 'firing' faculty members. On July 16, five hundred students and about twenty-five left-wing professors attended a meeting, presided over by Cubela, which abolished the University Council and set up a 'Superior Governing Board' composed of pro-Castro students and professors. Three weeks later the government legalized the board, and the autonomy of the university was a thing of the past."

Non-Communist professors were fired. "Of the eighty-five who were ousted from the Faculty of Medicine," says Dr. J. M. Portuondo, "at least fifty-five immediately became active in anti-Castro underground organizations."

Rafael Rodríguez, now editor of *Hoy*, was given the chair of political economy in the University's School of Social Sciences. Juan Marinello, head of the Cuban Communist Party, was appointed Rector of the University. "Higher education in Cuba," Comrade Rodríguez stated in August 1962, "would not correspond to the revolutionary process if university students did not receive an ideological training that would enable them to focus upon their life and political problems the scientific stereoscope that Marxism-Leninism affords us. Therefore, dialectical and historical materialism has been introduced into every course."

### *"Give Me the Children . . ."*

Ernesto Santamarina's married daughter, Señora Carlota Travieso, mother of three small children, came to see her father one day in May 1961. "Papa," she asked, "who was it said 'give me the children and I will guarantee that Communism will last forever'?"*

Santamarina looked startled. He was unfamiliar with the quotation but its implications made him think, with horror, of his grandchildren.

"I don't know," he admitted. "But why do you ask?"

"Because the words are true," Carlota said. "Papa, I am

* Lenin said: "Give me the children for four years and the seeds I have sown will never be uprooted."

going to take the children and leave Cuba. Pepe [her husband] would like to hold on a while longer, and I know you and Mama cannot leave as long as Grandmama lives. But we do not matter, Papa; we must think of the children. Their lives, their future, perhaps their immortal souls are in danger."

Then she explained: "Pepito [four] marches around singing the *Internationale* which he thinks is our national anthem. Where did he learn this? From his playmates, the children of some of our best friends. Manolo [seven] is angry because I will not allow him to join the Young Pioneers to which all his classmates belong. Yesterday Josefina [eleven] asked me what is a *prostituta*. Manolo had told that the nuns in her school are *prostitutas!* Do not look so shocked, Papa. Manolo says things even worse than that, things that our children are being taught deliberately. Their minds are being poisoned."

Thus, in the spring of 1961, the Travieso family joined the exodus from Cuba. The flight into exile began with the hasty departure of the *Batistianos* on January 1, 1959, then increased gradually almost as an index of the people's disenchantment with Fidel Castro. Businessmen and landowners, first to feel the whip of Communist economics, were soon followed by professional men and women—university professors, school teachers, lawyers, doctors, engineers. Toward the end of 1961 their number had reached 175,000. The later waves brought the "little people"—farmers, fishermen, cane-cutters, cattlehands, simple *guajiros*—many of whom couldn't afford plane fare and escaped in open boats which were picked up at sea or miraculously reached the Florida shores with the most wretched human cargoes U.S. Immigration officers had ever seen. The most common reason they gave for leaving Cuba was, "To save the children."

The exodus became a stampede in the fall of 1961 after the clandestine circulation within Cuba of a new law, *Pa-*

*tria Potestad* (State Custody), which was supposed to become effective on January 1, 1962. This provided that children between the ages of three and ten were to be placed in *Círculos Infantiles* (Child Centers); they would be allowed to see parents two days each month. After the age of ten, they would be transferred to centers in distant provinces. Moreover, after January 1, 1962, no minor would be allowed to leave Cuba without a special government permit.

Public reaction was hysterical. Whole families attempted to leave Cuba at any cost. Small children, unaccompanied by parents or guardians, were shipped out by their families and began to arrive in Miami at the rate of fifty to sixty a day. By early 1962 the flood of "unaccompanied minors" reached the 10,000 mark and created a puzzling problem for the U.S. government and private welfare agencies.

Whether the *Patria Potestad* draft was a fraud (as Castro claims), or whether the law was shelved because of its sensational implications is still debated. However, Ché Guevara, in dismissing the matter as anti-Castro propaganda, made several revealing admissions. "Since women in Cuba must work," he said, "and have less and less time to take care of children, it has been necessary to establish some *Círculos Infantiles*. . . . In remote places like the Sierra Maestra . . . we have thought it best for children to be educated in special centers. . . . The child would thus be separated from his family for a good many months a year [but] this is no worse than the rich people's boarding schools where children went eight or ten months without seeing their parents. . . ."

## *The New Cubans*

Many school teachers recognized the handwriting on the wall in Fidel Castro's early statement that no one over the age of thirty-five could be re-educated to "understand the revolution." Says Lidia Bermúdez, a Havana secondary school teacher: "Fidel's obsession with Cuban youth was understandable, since youth represents a nation's future. But he had his sights set on something more than a new generation of students; he wanted a new generation of teachers first. We soon learned that he was deadly serious when he said: 'The peasants will teach you the *why* of the revolution better than any book.' "

The education reform law passed in 1959 reshuffled the school system from primary grades through the university. It provided for new texts, curricula, teaching aids; reorganized the normal schools and set new standards for teacher training. "All that would take time," says Señorita Bermúdez, "and Fidel was in a hurry. The first stages he left to the indoctrinators and political organizers in his Ministry of Education, headed by Armando Hart."

Mariana Otero, a high school teacher in Camagüey, saw the changes begin in 1960: "First came the so-called 'student councils' formed by Communist-indoctrinated teachers and impressionable or revolutionary minded students. They organized study groups which met after school to discuss 'correct attitudes' toward the revolutionary program, agrarian reform, confiscation of private property, capitalism vs. communism, etc. Then pressure was put on all children to join the Young Pioneers and the Young Rebels which were amalgamations of the youth sections of the 26th of July Movement and those of the Communist Party (PSP). These youth groups with their uniforms, military drills, 'patriotic' songs, etc., had a tremendous appeal to small children and teen-agers. They gave the impressionable kids a steady diet of Communist propaganda in the form of lectures, films, and weekend trips to camps and 'recreation' centers. They instilled a blind and unquestioning devotion to the 'New Cuba' and hatred of the past and everything associated with the 'imperialist' world."

Through the study groups and youth organizations, the children were taught to spy on teachers and parents. They later became active agents in the "vigilante committees" which were organized in each neighborhood and city block. "They soon controlled the classrooms," says Señorita Bermúdez, "and discipline was impossible. By threatening to report the teacher to the authorities they exerted a form of blackmail to get good grades. Once a boy stole the record book from my desk. When I reported the incident the director told me to forget about it because the boy's father was an influential member of the Communist Party."

Señora Edenia Guillermo, for twenty years a social science teacher in the Vedado preparatory school, says that Young Rebels were taught to ask provocative questions in order to ferret out the possibly "counter-revolutionary" or "imperialistic" sympathies of the teachers. "For example, one had to be extremely careful," she says, "in responding to questions regarding the War of Independence and the Platt Amendment. One child might ask: 'Is it true that Estrada Palma [first President of Cuba] sold out to the Yankee imperialists?' One had to bear in mind that Estrada Palma, like many other Cuban patriots, was being 'downgraded' by the new regime.

"One of my oldest friends, a highly respected history teacher, made the mistake of saying that living standards were higher in the United States and pre-revolutionary Cuba than in the Soviet Union. She was bombarded thereafter by tricky and 'incriminating' questions and became involved in so much trouble with the school authorities that she was forced to seek asylum in an embassy and leave Cuba."

Angela Toledo finished high school in Camagüey in the spring of 1960 as an honor student and was offered a scholarship in the Soviet Union or any Soviet-bloc country of her choice. "They painted a very alluring picture," she says. "My passage and all expenses would be paid, a suitable wardrobe would be furnished, and I would receive a monthly stipend. I replied, truthfully, that my ambition had always been to study medicine at the University of Havana.

"They finally agreed to this, but told me that, because I was not yet eighteen, it would be easier for me to be admitted to the university if I could present a letter of sponsorship from a member of the Communist Party. I would also have to enlist in the student militia and join certain other groups. Rather than become involved politically, I gave up the idea of going to Havana, using as an excuse the illness of my father.

"Instead, I remained in Camagüey and studied to become a teacher of physical education. Unfortunately, I ran head-on into Fidel's 'literacy' campaign and soon found myself assigned to training *alfabetizadores* (teachers of illiterates) who were illiterate themselves."

### *The Magic of A-B-C*

Fidel Castro had proclaimed 1961 "The Year of Education." Primary and secondary schools would be closed from April to December; teachers and pupils alike would devote their time to teaching illiterate Cubans how to read and write.

"Actually, there was illiteracy in Cuba," says Señora Guillermo. "But the illiteracy rate, according to the 1953 census, was twenty-three per cent, lowest in Latin America with the exception of Argentina, Costa Rica and Chile. The rate was lowest (eleven per cent) in the cities, highest (forty-one per cent) in the rural areas. Speaking before the United Nations in 1960, Castro resorted to the 'Big Lie' and stated that Cuba was forty per cent illiterate—over

2,000,000 people. He had to scale down those figures before his *alfabetizacion* campaign ended."

Early in 1961 posters appeared in Cuban offices, factories, hospitals and public buildings appealing for volunteer teachers: "Lounge on beautiful beaches while performing your revolutionary duty. . . . Live in the luxurious homes of the capitalists while you *alfabetize*."

Angela Toledo was assigned to train a "literacy brigade" at Varadero Beach. "Over 80,000 trainees passed through the center between June and the beginning of the campaign in September," she says. "Besides the teachers and the school children (ten to eighteen years) there were clerks, mechanics, nurses, laborers who were attracted by the promises of an easy life. They drew their regular salaries plus board and keep. At Varadero Beach, we gave them a 'cram course' in teaching, using the paperback primers they would use on the job. This, of course, was pure propaganda."

When the training period ended, the fledgling "teachers" were assigned to posts in the rural areas. Ernesto Torre, eighteen years old, was sent with a group to the Sierra Cristal in northern Oriente province. "At first, I was enthusiastic about the program," he says, "but I was quickly disillusioned. We worked all day with the farmers, eating whatever they ate. We held our classes at night. You didn't have to be very smart to see that it was all propaganda and indoctrination. Even the illiterate *campesinos* saw through it. One old fellow said angrily: 'I don't want to know what the book *says*. I want to learn to read and write.' "

Like most Cubans who went through the experience and are willing to talk about it, Ernesto Torre mentions the immorality in the ABC camps. "There was wide-open promiscuity," he says. "We had some pretty bad characters in our group—former prostitutes, gangsters, gamblers and a few drug addicts. This had a terrible effect on some of the youngsters in the program who had never seen such things."

Beatriz Medina, who joined the program as a teacher while in her first year of normal school, says, "Any boy and girl who wished to spend the night together were free to do so, and with the camp commander's blessing. Many girls became pregnant. If they were under fifteen, an abortion was arranged; if they were older, they could have the baby or an abortion, as they wished."

Doctors from Havana, Santa Clara, Santiago and other large cities substantiate these stories. "Castro's 'Year of Education' should have been called the 'Year of Maternity,'" says a Santiago physician. A Havana obstetrician says: "We had to set up a special ward in the university hospital to take care of these girls. I might also add that, in all my years of practice in public clinics, I have never seen so many cases of advanced venereal disease."

The ABC campaign was a dismal failure, which even the government was unable to hide. The target figure of "two-million new literates by January" was eventually scaled down to 980,000. Even this was considered an exaggeration by professional teachers who participated in the program.

"I enjoyed teaching a class of stevedores," says Mariana Otero, "because they really wanted to learn. But they barely could copy letters from the book, and only a few learned to write their names. When the campaign ended, I was asked to certify that those in my class could read and write. I refused. I was reprimanded several times, and in January and February my salary checks were withheld. Finally, I was forced out of my regular teaching job in March."

The tragic experiment was not without humerous aspects. As a fitting climax to the course, each pupil was required to write a "Thank you Fidel" letter to the great educator. "Usually, these letters had to be written with the teacher practically guiding the pupil's hand," says Angela Toledo. "Often the misspellings or an unwitting play on words were so funny that we just allowed the letters to pass."

The story is told that in Pinar del Río an old peasant, who barely learned to read and write, was rewarded at the graduation ceremony with the gift of a horse. Around the horse's neck hung a sign with the revolutionary slogan, "*Patria o Muerte*" (Fatherland or Death). After "reading" the sign he refused the gift contemptuously. "Who wants a horse that kicks and bites [*Patea y Muerde*]?" he asked.

### *New Texts—and New Teachers*

The nine-month recess for the ABC program gave the regime time to implement the long-range program. When the schools reopened in January 1962 there were new texts, new programs—and new teachers. Those teachers who had not participated in the literacy program had been fired. Other teachers, disillusioned by the ABC fiasco and angered by the new "teachers' unions" they were forced to join, resigned in droves.

"The union in my district," says a teacher in the Vedado section of Havana, "was made up largely of clerks, cleaning women and janitors. Only 26 out of 108 teachers signed up. However, in other parts of Cuba, where the pressures were greater, about sixty per cent of the teachers joined although they no longer had any pride in the profession."

The resulting teacher shortage did not faze the regime. Students, some of whom had not finished high school, replaced the professional teachers. The only requisite was that they be party members or had completed an indoctrination course.

The old textbooks had been withdrawn and destroyed. "New texts had been prepared," says Señora Guillermo.

"They were full of propaganda. The history text for secondary schools, *Cuba Under the Socialist Revolution*, omitted or maligned Cuban patriots. Carlos Manuel de Céspedus, hero of the War of Independence, was presented as a large landowner who went to war only to protect his own interests; Narciso López, another patriot, was a 'mercenary' paid by the imperialists, etc. Even the Spanish grammar book was full of propaganda."

Evidence of the new objectives of education appeared in the official Ministry of Education Program for 1962. The pre-school (kindergarten) "Objectives of Education" states the aims: "To educate the new generation so that they may participate actively and conscientiously in the building of the Socialist State. . . . To instill self-discipline and conduct favorable to the norms of a socialist society. . . . To strengthen the will and form the character of children in order that they may conquer the difficulties created by imperialistic forces. . . ." Secondary school social studies stress the "Socialist Revolution and Dictatorship of the Proletariat. . . . Correlation of Armed Force and Peaceful Forms in the Battle for Power. . . . Coexistence—the Inevitable Victory of Socialism."

Between 50,000 and 80,000 hand-picked *becados* (state scholars) are now being trained as Communist indoctrinators in new "Schools of Revolutionary Education." In November 1962, Leonel Soto, director of the program, described the schools in the party magazine, *Cuba Socialista:* "We must train cultural cadres who will be with the revolution all the way. . . . Admission to these schools is not subject to passing an entrance examination. . . . Students must be selected from among revolutionary cadres and activists—those who distinguish themselves in the struggle. . . . Study material is the classics of Marxism-Leninism, books and pamphlets. . . . Nobody but Marxists are graduated. . . . Thousands of graduates are being assigned to leadership of study circles at various levels. . . .

The Revolution requires that this effort be intensified and improved."

The skill and avidity with which Communist Cuba adhered to Lenin's claim ("Give me the children for four years . . .") caused many Cuban educators to despair of what must be done if and when Cuba is liberated. "The problem of re-orienting the children to democracy will be especially difficult," says James D. Baker, former headmaster of Ruston Academy, an outstanding private coeducational school in Havana. "In June 1960, confidential information from within the government showed that Fidel Castro realized that he might be overthrown. He made plans then for a later return to power in case of a temporary defeat. Communist leaders showed that they were fully aware that the future of the regime rests upon the success of their programs for indoctrinating children.

"Closing the schools for nine months in 1961 for the purpose of teaching illiterates was only a pretext; the real purpose was to submit large groups of youngsters to brainwashing, and to delay the resumption of regular classes until teachers could be screened, reoriented or trained for their new tasks.

"Since then the indoctrination programs have been accelerated. The Young Pioneers and Communist youth organizations now control and direct children from the ages of six to sixteen, after which they pass into the militia. The people in charge of these groups have been thoroughly trained in Soviet methods of indoctrination. For the first two years Castro was in power his 'Hate the U.S.' campaign had little effect except upon the rabble who followed him blindly. Since 1961, however, the program has produced disturbing results.

"The problem is well illustrated by this story told by a Cuban mother. A few days after the family arrived in Miami, her six-year-old son was greatly upset when he learned that the aunt with whom they were living was a citizen of the United States. 'Then we will have to kill her!' the boy said. 'Fidel told us that we must kill all Americans!'

"Salvaging that lad's generation, I believe, will be the greatest task which Cubans will have to face after the liberation."

### *Castro Tackles the Church*

The churchmen in predominantly Catholic Cuba were as thoroughly hoodwinked by Fidel Castro's communism as were the majority of laymen.

Shortly after his shattering experience with the regime's firing squads in January 1959, Father Jorge Bez Chabebe, the Catholic Youth chaplain in Santiago, went to Havana to consult his superiors. He complained that too many priests were being gulled by Castro's false promises. He recommended that the church set up a commission to investigate the communistic trend of the new regime. To his astonishment, his suggestions were brushed aside. The hierarchy, like the majority of Cubans, refused to believe that Castro was a Communist. Fidel's program, particularly the agrarian reform, was deemed sound and worthy. The Communists around Castro were looked upon as parasites who inevitably attach themselves to any democratic government.

Late in 1959, a tract entitled "The Catholic Church and Cuba," written in Spanish but printed in Peking, was circulated confidentially to Castro officials and the party faithful. The author, Li Wei Han, warned that the Roman Catholic Church "is a source of counter-revolutionary activities in all people's democracies. This is the program of tactics we used successfully in the People's Republic of China to liberate the Chinese people from the influence of the church and the imperialists of Rome."

Li Wei Han urged Cuba to move swiftly but cautiously, and to avoid frontal attacks—"do not make martyrs." Failure to consider the "acute psychological struggle," he said, may "alienate the [Catholic] masses from the Party." He recommended setting up a government agency to direct "steps which will weaken the church and degrade its image." Organize Cuban Catholics into "patriotic groups," and these groups will antagonize and identify "counter-revolutionary" Catholic leaders who "must be eliminated with firmness but without violence," he wrote.

"The tactic of two paces forward, and then one backward must be used," Li Wei Han warned. "Declare that the government defends religious liberty. Convince the masses that they can have their religion without the Vatican. Activists [Communist leaders] have the important duty of persuading the ecclesiastical authorities to make similar declarations. . . . Thus the way is prepared for establishment of an independent church . . . free from elements that continue to have relations with the Vatican. . . . Then we can consecrate our own church leaders. . . . The masses will notice little difference [as] we proceed with a gradual uprooting of these elements in the liturgy that are incompatible with the popular government. . . ."

Fidel Castro tried to implement the Chinese plan but was unable to master the cautious tactic of "two steps forward, one backward." He personally tried to interest several priests, including the popular Father Juan O'Farril and Father Eduardo Aguirre, in establishing a Cuban Catholic Church; when they refused and fled Cuba, Fidel denounced them as "Judases" and "vultures."

"Castro then turned the job over to Señor Antonio Pruna," says Father Jorge. "Pruna, a Havana businessman, came to me early in 1960 posing as a Catholic leader and Cuban patriot. His argument was that a national church would enable the Cuban clergy to get rid of the Spanish priests who were then a majority. He asked me to think it over and discuss it with my colleague, Father Rivas. Instead, I went to Havana and reported the incident to the Bishop."

The "national church" plan was soon dropped for lack of clerical cooperation. But a spectacular effort was made to lure Cuban Catholics into a "patriotic" movement known as "With Cross and with Fatherland." The leading figures were Father Germán Lence, a fat, ineffectual priest who had been suspended by the Archbishop of Santiago; Father Rafael Sardiñas, a shadowy figure who had served as a chaplain in the Sierra Maestra, and wore an olive-green cassock with epaulets and a major's insignia; and Señora Lula Horstmann, a tall, mannish woman in her fifties, who acted as leader of the women's division.

"The 'Cross and Fatherland' movement," says Father Jorge, "was launched in February 1960 with a televised 'mass' in a Havana park with Father Lence officiating. Despite the tremendous advance publicity by the government propagandists, the affair was poorly attended. Watching it on television you could tell that most of those in the crowd were not regular churchgoers because they did not know how to behave. Father Lence, who is a poor speaker with a weak voice, preached a brief 'sermon' in which he extolled the revolution and attacked 'reactionary' and 'imperialistic' Catholics. The whole thing lasted less than forty-five minutes."

Elsewhere in Cuba, "Cross and Fatherland" rallies were larger and better attended. But the organized mobs got out of hand and attacked priests and Catholic laymen who defended the Church. Castro then resorted to divisive tactics. He said that there were "good priests" and "bad priests," a "high clergy" which was Falangist and imperialist, and a "low clergy" which was made up of humble priests who were patriotic Cubans. When he attacked the nuns of the Sacred Heart School, he added piously:

"This does not mean that all nuns, all priests, are counter-revolutionaries. I know many nuns who work, who are humble, and who are revolutionaries, just as there are priests who are revolutionaries, and others who are among the worst."

Yet everything that Castro tried backfired. "He even adopted the old Communist trick," says Father Manuel Aguirre, "of having men wearing cassocks frequent the cabarets, night clubs and brothels of Havana. They were seen strolling along the streets arm-in-arm with well-known prostitutes. This despicable tactic failed when the clergy exposed and denounced it from the pulpits."

### *"Social Justice, Sí! Comunismo, No!"*

The Catholic clergy's uneasy tolerance of the Castro regime ended soon after the CTC convention of November 1959, when the Communists seized control of the labor movement and ousted Catholic leaders from the Cuban unions.

On November 29, 1959, hundreds of thousands of Cubans flocked to Havana for the first National Catholic Congress. To avoid trouble with the regime, the speakers were chosen carefully and their speeches were censored in advance by the hierarchy. But a modest statement made by Dr. José Ignacio Lasaga, clinical psychologist and a leader of the Catholic Youth Movement, provided the spark that set off a popular explosion.

"We believe," he said, "that the Catholic attitude toward the revolution can be summed up in this phrase: 'Social Justice, Yes! Communism, No!' "

"The roar that went up from the crowded Tropical Stadium," says Dr. Lasaga, "astonished me and, I am sure, the many dignitaries present. Then the people began to chant: 'Cuba, Yes! Russia, No!' They put on a tremendous demonstration. It was all so spontaneous and unexpected

—the first loud, popular outcry against communism in Cuba."

Fidel Castro reacted angrily. "This is dishonest and unjust," he declared. "They are even using the Virgin of Charity [patron saint of Cuba] to attack the revolution. Hundreds of thousands of Cubans are attending the congress to pray for Cuba and the revolution."

On May 16, 1960, the first pastoral letter denouncing communism ("The enemy is already within our gates!") was issued by the seventy-six-year-old Archbishop of Santiago, Monsignor Enrique Pérez Serantes, whose intervention with Batista had saved Castro's life after the 1953 attack on the Moncada Barracks. Says Father Francisco Villaverde of Havana: "Now many priests began preaching openly about the dangers of communism, reminding parishioners of what had happened in the Soviet-bloc countries, and pointing to the deadly parallel in what was happening in Cuba."

The Castro regime declared open warfare on the church. "The Catholics have nothing to fear," said Juan Marinello, president of the Communist Party, "so long as they remain in their temples adoring their images. But if they leave their temples and work in the counter-revolution, they will find us in the front line fighting against them."

The violence began in July 17, 1960, when a mass for victims of communism was celebrated in the cathedral of Havana. Señora Renée Peyrera, gives this eyewitness account: "The cathedral was crowded to overflowing. But when Monsignor Boza Masvidal [Auxiliary Archbishop of Havana] preached the sermon few could hear him because someone had tampered with the amplifying system. When the Mass ended everyone sang 'Viva Cristo Rey' [Long Live Christ the King], then the women waved their handkerchiefs and began singing the national anthem.

We could hear the mob outside shouting ins[illegible] singing the 'Internationale.' As the crowd emer[illegible] the cathedral, the militiamen, who were suppose[illegible] to preserve order, provoked a fight and the rioting starte[illegible] People were picked at random and arrested as the provocateurs; probably more would have been taken had not the angry congregation outnumbered the militia. But the police did take the license numbers of cars and more people were picked up later."

More attacks on churches followed. Militiamen, bearing arms, marched in during Mass and shouted revolutionary slogans during sermons. On August 8, 1960, the Church issued a collective pastoral message, signed by all bishops, which stated: "Catholicism and communism [are] two concepts of man and the world that are totally opposed and can never be reconciled. . . . Remember, our children, and say it loudly to all Cuba, that the Church fears nothing from the most profound social reforms as long as they are based on justice and charity. . . . But precisely because [the Church] loves people and wants their good, it can do no less than condemn Communist doctrines. . . . The majority of the Cuban people, which is Catholic, is against materialistic and atheistic communism. Only by deceit or coercion could the Cuban people be led into a Communist regime. . . ."

### *To the Catacombs*

The abortive invasion of April 1961 gave Fidel Castro the perfect pretext to move in for the kill. Churches, convents, and schools were raided and looted by militiamen. Altars were profaned, the sacred Hosts were scattered on the floor and trampled upon, statues and relics were smashed, chalices and jeweled crucifixes were stolen. In Camagüey, militiamen got drunk on sacramental wine, staged mock weddings, and then, after desecrating the altars, paraded through the streets holding aloft sacred vessels and dancing to the rhythm of the cha-cha-cha.

The wholesale arrests of Catholic priests began on the morning of April 17. Four of the six bishops were imprisoned. The Bishop of Camagüey, whose ring and pectoral cross were torn from him, managed to escape from the barracks where he was interned. The Vicar General of Pinar del Río was searched and photographed against a background of pornographic books and pictures. Castro's onetime benefactor, Archbishop Pérez Serantes, aged and infirm, was given the opportunity to escape but preferred house arrest. He told a colleague: "I will leave Cuba only as a corpse."

September 8, 1961, marked the Feast of the Virgin of Charity, patron saint of Cuba. Fidel Castro prohibited the customary processions. But, because of the stubborn insistence of Bishop Boza Masvidal, the Ministry of Interior granted permission to celebrate the feast inside the Church of Our Lady of Charity in Havana on Sunday, September 10.

"The multitude filled the church and the streets for several blocks around," says Father Villaverde. "The crowds outside became angry and began to shout for the traditional procession. The militia seemed unable to cope with the situation, so reserves were rushed to the church, under the command of Major Ramiro Valdés, the Minister of Interior, who appeared wearing a Russian military cap adorned with hammer-and-sickle insignia.

"The militiamen charged against the demonstrators swinging clubs and firing machine guns. Many were wounded, and one boy, Arnaldo Socorro, a devout Catholic and a leader of the Young Catholic Workers' Association, was killed. The next day Fidel Castro proclaimed young Socorro a 'hero of the revolution' who had been shot down by priests!"

The reprisals started immediately. More churches and

convents were raided and priests and nuns arrested. On September 12, about one hundred and thirty-five priests were herded aboard the Spanish steamer *Covadonga.* At the last minute, the sailing was delayed for one final passenger, and Monsignor Boza Masvidal was rudely shoved aboard.

Fidel Castro announced over a national television network on September 19, 1961, that religious demonstrations would never again be permitted in Cuba. He also declared that Cuban priests who did not pledge their loyalty to the regime would be deprived of their citizenship and be deported.

Father Diego Madrigal, formerly of Our Lady of Charity Church in Havana, was one of the many priests who refused to genuflect to communism. "One night I was hauled out of bed," he says, "and placed aboard a ship in Havana harbor along with more than one hundred other priests. We landed in Spain, then we went our separate ways to the United States, Puerto Rico, Venezuela and other Latin American countries. Today, there are only about one hundred and twenty priests left in Cuba to minister to nearly 6,000,000 Catholics. Much as in the early days of the Roman persecution, Christ's church in Cuba is in the catacombs."

# Part Six

# EXPORTING THE REVOLUTION

On July 26, 1960, Fidel Castro, celebrating the seventh anniversary of his attack on the Moncada Barracks, boasted: "We promise to continue making [Cuba] the example that can convert the Cordillera of the Andes into the Sierra Maestra of the American continent."

Dr. Nicolás Rivero, who was then a disillusioned officer in the Ministry of Foreign Relations, says: "I wondered how many nations in the Western Hemisphere, both the people and their governments, would grasp the significance of that bold admission. Here was the real meaning, the most serious threat, of the Castro revolution. The revolution meant more than communism in Cuba. The ultimate goal was the Sovietization of the hemisphere. The Cuban revolution was made for export purposes. We were already exporting it, and we had been exporting it very efficiently ever since Mikoyan's visit in February."

Dr. Rivero adds solemnly: "Few Americans were listening, fewer still caught the significance and realized the danger. They don't realize it even today, despite the evidence that has been disclosed in the Caribbean, Central and South America. The Soviet military and economic build-up of Cuba always was 'defensive' in one sense only. The Soviet Union had to strengthen and defend its Cuban satellite because only from Cuba, the strategic beachhead, can Russia communize Latin America and, ultimately, the Western Hemisphere."

Castro's first bumbling attempts to "export the revolution" by armed invasions of Panama, Nicaragua, Haiti and the Dominican Republic in 1959 were abandoned after the Mikoyan visit and the subsequent arrival in Havana in

March 1960 of Alexei Alekseyev and his corps of trained technicians from the Kremlin's Latin American section. Under Russian guidance the Cuban Foreign Service was purged of career officers who had served under previous regimes. These were supplanted by reliable but unknown Cuban Communists.

"No one else was acceptable," says Dr. Rivero. "My first attempt to leave Cuba was to apply for a post in Latin America. I was offered assignments in several of the African republics, but I was told that Latin America was out of the question. I understood why when I saw the men who were being groomed for assignment to the American republics. They were all hardened, dedicated Communists."

From the beginning, the director-general of Cuban operations in the Kremlin's plan to "export the revolution" was Major Ernesto (Ché) Guevara. As early as June 1959 he declared publicly: "We have demonstrated that a small group of determined men supported by the people and not afraid to die if necessary, can overwhelm a regular disciplined army and defeat it definitely. That is the fundamental lesson. There is another which should be learned by our brothers of Latin America, who find themselves economically in the same agrarian category as ourselves, and that is that they must undertake an agrarian revolution, fight in the fields and in the mountains, and from there carry the revolution to the cities. . . ."

Later, in 1960, after a tour of the Communist nations, Guevara stated frankly why Russia and China were eager to give Cuba economic assistance: "They consider that the example of Cuba is helping Latin America very much to repeat what happened in Cuba, and in the measure that the Cuban example is repeated, to that extent imperialism will be denied sources [of raw materials]. Thus, naturally, imperialism's power of aggression will be weakened."

During a visit to China in November 1960, Guevara

discussed with Premier Chou En-lai a joint communiqué announcing China's offer of 60 million dollars in credit to be paid over 15 years. The words "disinterested aid by the socialist countries" in the Cuban draft rankled the Chinese.

"They refused absolutely to accept the word 'disinterested,'" Guevara reported. "They said that they were giving aid, but it was *interested* aid. Because Cuba at this moment is one of the countries in the vanguard of the struggle against imperialism. Imperialism is the common enemy of all people; therefore, aid to Cuba is in the interest of all socialist countries."

Guevara agreed that the word "disinterested" should be deleted. "They are right when they say it is not disinterested," he said. "It is aid which permits us to maintain ourselves in the vanguard of the struggle against North American imperialism."

### *Operation America*

Guevara went on to Moscow in December 1960 to attend the gathering of 81 Communist parties from all over the world. This was one of the most important meetings ever held by the top-level representatives of the Communist international apparatus. Special attention was given to Latin America. "Operation America" henceforth would be directed exclusively from the Kremlin. Plans were made to set up a network of secret radio transmitters, schools for agents and liaison personnel, workshops for the counterfeiting of currency and documents, and to promote the traffic in narcotics when it would serve the Communist cause.

As far back as 1957, Latin American Communists had held high-level conferences in Moscow following meetings of world-wide heads of Communist parties. Directly out of these conclaves had come the decision to maintain headquarters in Mexico City to coordinate Communist propaganda and to aid Cuba. Then, in February 1959, Latin Communist leaders attending the 21st Party Congress decided that it would be more expedient to use Cuba as a base in the future. The Cuban Comrades were instructed to penetrate non-Communist parties and revolutionary groups and thus gain control of "popular" revolutions in Latin America.

Guevara was ecstatic when this directive was confirmed and amplified at the 1960 meeting. While still in Moscow, he declared that it was "one of the most important events of recent times." He boasted that the official declaration reaffirming the Sino-Soviet goal of communizing the world had mentioned Cuba no less than four times. The Castro regime was proclaimed a "powerful stimulus to the struggle of the Latin American peoples for complete national liberation."

Shortly thereafter, Castro's propaganda machine was overhauled by Soviet experts. Prensa Latina, the government-controlled news agency, became a streamlined, Spanish-language model of Tass, the Kremlin's wire service, and like Tass it serves not only as a medium for Communist propaganda but as a front for subversive activities and espionage. Argentina and Perú soon barred the Prensa Latina service to national newspapers and broadcasters; but the agency continued to operate legally in seven other Latin American countries.

Tons of printed propaganda began to pour regularly into Latin America from Cuba, most of it printed on the presses of the democratic newspapers and magazines that had been forced to flee Cuba. This material ranges from handbills and leaflets to lavishly printed four-color magazines. Early in 1961, the director of Imprenta Nacional, the government printing agency, visited both the Soviet Union and Red China where he made arrangements for the publication in Spanish of Russian and Chinese works for distribution in Latin America. Since then Imprenta Nacional has issued over 250,000 volumes of the works of Mao Tse-tung alone.

## *How to Make a Revolution*

But the most popular Cuban book exported to Latin America appears to be the 187-page manual on guerrilla warfare (*Guerra de Guerrillas*) by Ché Guevara. First published in Havana in April 1960 by the Department of Instructions of the Ministry of Armed Forces, Guevara's book is a blueprint for revolution—a lucidly written do-it-yourself-manual on how to begin with 30 to 50 men and overturn a government. Based mainly on Ché's experience in the Sierra Maestra, this book provides a formula which, if properly applied, could repeat the Cuban tragedy in Latin America regardless of local sentiment or the numerical weakness of Communists.

Guevara hammers at the point that what happened in Cuba can happen anywhere in Latin America. It is not necessary to wait for the development of all underlying conditions for the revolution, he maintains: "the forces of insurrection can create them."

"The guerrilla," says Guevara, "is above all an agrarian revolutionary. Mao Tse-tung's China began with workers' uprisings that were defeated and almost wiped out. It recovered only when it concentrated in rural areas and adopted the cause of agrarian reform.

"There is a saying: 'The guerrilla is the maverick of war.' He practices deception, treachery, surprise, and night operations. Thus, circumstances and the 'will to win' often oblige him to forget romantic and sportsmanlike concepts. Military strategy and tactics represent the way the group achieves its objectives by taking full advantage of the enemy's weak points.

"A major responsibility of guerrilla leaders is the proper

choice of the time and place to defend the positions to the end. If a first-class terrain study finds an impregnable position in the path of the enemy's advance, he can be stopped cold by just a few guerrillas. The way a guerrilla army attacks also is different: a sudden, surprise, furious, relentless attack; then, abruptly, total passivity. The survivors think things have returned to normal, when suddenly a fresh blow lands from a new direction. An unexpected lightning blow is what counts.

"The importance of suburban fighting has not been fully appreciated. When done effectively and extended over a wide area, it completely paralyzes the everyday life of the sector. The population becomes restless, anguished, almost anxious for the development of violence, in order to bring the matter to an end. If, at the very start of the war, specialists are organized for suburban guerrilla work, quicker action can be obtained, more lives spared, and the nation's valuable time saved.

"To attain the stature of a true crusader, the guerrilla must display impeccable moral conduct and strict self-control. He must be an ascetic. At first, he will not stress social reform, acting more as a big brother to the poor farmer in matters of technology, economics, morals, and culture.

"The local population must be won over through help and sympathy. Anyone who takes advantage of a chaotic situation and exploits the local population must be punished. In other words, all who sympathize with the revolutionary movement must be treated well; all those who attack the movement, sow dissension, or betray the guerrillas must be dealt with harshly.

"Women can play an extraordinarily important role in the development of a revolutionary process. They are capable of the most difficult deeds, of fighting with the troops, and they do not cause sexual conflicts among the troops, as has been charged. They should be entrusted with carrying confidential messages, ammunition, etc. If captured, they will invariably be better treated than men no matter how brutal the enemy. They can cook for the troops and perform other duties of a domestic nature, teach the soldiers and the local population, indoctrinate the children, perform the functions of social workers, nurse the sick, help sew uniforms, and, if necessary, even bear arms. Use women to infiltrate the enemy camp. Use trained men and women to spread rumors and sow confusion and fear among the enemy."

On indoctrination and training, Guevara says: "Since recruits join up with fuzzy concepts of liberty, freedom of the press, etc., they need indoctrination on guerrilla aims, economic factors and motivations of national history, national heroes, behavior in the face of injustice, analysis of the current situation. Set up teacher training centers and prepare textbooks for indoctrination. Encourage reading and supervise the choice of books. Above all, inculcate a reasoning, not a mechanical, self-discipline. This is the best assurance for success when the chips are down in combat. . . .

"Absolute secrecy is crucial. One has to make do with those who are available—exiles and volunteers eager to join the fight for liberation. Yet there is no excuse for intelligence reaching the enemy, even if the guerrilla organization has been infiltrated by spies, for no more than one or two persons should be familiar with preparatory plans. Keep new volunteers away from key places.

"Absolutely nobody must learn anything beyond his immediate concern. Trust no one beyond the nucleus, especially not women. The enemy will undoubtedly try to use women for espionage. [Therefore] the revolutionary, secretly preparing for war, must be an ascetic and perfectly disciplined. Anyone who repeatedly defies the orders of his superior and makes contact with women and other outsiders, however innocuous, must be expelled immediately for violation of revolutionary discipline."

Toward the end of his book Guevara hands out advice on what to do when the battle has been won. The words obviously apply to what happened in Cuba. "Final liberation comes only with the total systematic breakup of the enemy army and all institutions that supported the old regime. Therefore, no trace of the old army and its soldiers can remain. Militarism, blind obedience, old concepts of military duty, discipline and morale cannot be uprooted as long as the victors—noble, good, but generally uneducated—tolerate the defeated—well-trained, knowledgeable in the war of sciences, full of hatred against the guerrillas.

"Revolutionary action must be rededicated by forging a new army with technical skill, unshakable ideology, and great combat power. At this stage, begin to prepare for the new defensive war the people's army may have to fight. In the wake of victory, thousands of belated revolutionaries will want to join. These will have to undergo guerrilla-warfare training and indoctrination. Set up a propaganda organization to disseminate the new truths about the revolution among army units. Carry the campaign to the soldiers, the rural population, the workers. Forge the new army into a highly skilled force with a solid ideology and great combat power."

Guevara's text, however, was not the only guerrilla manual circulating in Latin American revolutionary circles. In northeastern Brazil, a Peiping-printed handbook of selections from the articles, books and speeches of Mao Tse-tung, entitled *Tactics of Guerrilla Fighters,* has had wide distribution. Another clandestine publication is *One Hundred and Fifty Questions and Answers for Guerrillas* by General Alberto Bayo, the man who taught Fidel his first lessons in guerrilla tactics in Mexico and is now training Latin American revolutionaries in Cuba.

### *Guerrillas, Spies and Saboteurs*

Beginning in late 1960, Cuban embassies and consulates in Latin America were enlarged and staffed with hand-picked men. They ceased to be conventional diplomatic missions, and became Soviet-style centers for propaganda, espionage and political agitation. They established contact with university students, labor leaders, editors and journalists, dissident and revolutionary political groups and, of course, the Communist parties (legal and illegal). Special emphasis was given to the formation of "fronts" and "friendship societies." By the end of 1961 a total of 51 such societies had been organized in 13 Central and South American countries. An important function of these groups was to take over the embassy's undercover work in the event that diplomatic relations with Cuba were suspended.

Meanwhile, training schools for Latin American revolutionists were set up in Cuba. "Trainees are recruited by the local committees and fronts," says Pedro Roig, who defected from the Cuban Embassy in Mexico City in June 1962. "When they are approved by the embassy G-2 agent, passage is arranged, usually via Mexico or some other country from which they can enter and leave Havana as 'tourists' without the Cuban stopover showing on their passports. Many also leave their country illegally on false passports provided by the Cubans.

"The training usually is a clue to the Cuban estimate of how the revolution can succeed in a particular country. For example, Argentines, Mexicans and Peruvians are schooled primarily in political techniques, with a minimum of military and guerrilla training, because of the planned strategy to take over those countries by political infiltration. On the other hand, students from Venezuela, Costa Rica, Nicaragua, Guatemala and the Dominican

Republic, which probably will have to be taken by armed struggle, go to a guerrilla training school such as those at Minas del Frío, San Julián and Minas de Francisco, which are under the direction of General Enrique Líster Forjan, Loyalist veteran of the Spanish Civil War.

"This strategy in training was exemplified in the case of Panama, which broke diplomatic relations with Cuba in December 1961. Panamanians who were in the Cuban political warfare schools, in preparation for operations in the 'national liberation front' were hastily transferred to Minas del Frío for intensive training in sabotage and guerrilla warfare. This was a victory for the Panamanian 'Vanguard of National Action.' The VAN had consistently favored an armed struggle in Panama, but was opposed by the Panamanian Communist Party which was committed to the political approach."

Confidential reports compiled by anti-Castro Cubans in Central and South America in 1961 cite by name several hundred Latin American Communists who completed their training in Cuba and now are operating in their native lands. Some examples:

• Tulio Bayer Jaramillo arrived in Cuba early in 1961, on a false passport, completed his training, and by the following October was leader of a guerrilla band operating in the Vichada River area of Colombia. Weapons used by Bayer's guerrillas were bought with Cuban funds in Curaçao and shipped to Colombia via Venezuela.

• Manuel Gómez Flores, former officer of the Nicaraguan National Guard, was running a guerrilla training school for 150 revolutionaries in Punta Llorona, Costa Rica, with the aid of several Cubans. Moreover, 15 Costa Ricans were sent to Cuba in August 1961 by Andres Armona Ramos, chargé d'affaires and G-2 agent in the Cuban Embassy in San José. The Costa Rican graduates boast that they were trained personally by General Enrique Líster.

• The Communist Party in Caracas in October 1961 sent a group of non-Communist but leftist Venezuelan labor leaders to Cuba for political training. The party leaders reported that the Venezuelan fellow-travelers "are more cooperative" as a result of their Cuban experience and that the program would be continued.

• Two Peruvian Communist leaders were brought to Cuba in August 1961 by Hilda Gadea, former wife of Ché Guevara. While they were in Cuba, they had meetings with Fidel Castro, Blas Roca, and Juan Marinello at which plans were made for the formation of a new "party of the masses" in Perú which would have no connection with the Peruvian Communist Party (PSP). Castro stressed the importance of training the peasants for revolutionary activities and offered to send instructors to Perú.

• In accordance with Ché Guevara's contention that "women can play an extraordinarily important role in the revolutionary process," a school near Havana, staffed entirely by Soviet instructors, offers women revolutionaries an eight-month course in espionage, sabotage, medicine, psychology, and investigation. Some 1961 graduates: Elisa Romero Martínez of El Salvador; Hemila Lila Corradi, Uruguay; and Gladys Feijóo, Communist women's leader in Perú.

### *Fiasco in Nicaragua*

In August 1961, Antonio Sikaffy, of unknown nationality but traveling on a Honduran passport, left Havana for Honduras with funds to finance revolutionary operations in both Honduras and Nicaragua. In September, Julio Mayorga, a Nicaraguan revolutionary, had the misfortune to be nabbed by police at the Managua, Nicaragua, airport with the sum of $3,600 on him. His confession revealed that Sikaffy was a Cuban courier engaged in distributing funds to agents of the United Nicaraguan Front (FUN) for a Castro-financed invasion of Nicaragua.

Mayorga's confession led to the disclosure that the Communist-dominated FUN, which maintained branches in Havana, Caracas and Honduras, planned to invade Nicaragua from Honduras and Costa Rica in November 1961. Arms purchased in Honduras had already been shipped into Nicaragua. The master plan, drawn up in Havana, called for the revolt to begin with the assassination of General Anastasio Somoza, chief of Nicaragua's armed forces, an attack on the U.S. Embassy, and the bombing of Managua. Bombers, based in Honduras, were to be painted dark gray and without distinctive markings. Internal uprisings and sabotage were to be carried out by the Juventud Patriótica (the name the FUN operated under in Nicaragua) with arms and explosives already hidden within Nicaragua.

The plan called for a simultaneous uprising in Honduras against the government of José Ramón Villeda (Morales) which would make it difficult for Honduras to detain the Nicaraguan invaders. Also, the Costa Rican Communists and members of the Friends of the Cuban Revolution were warned by Havana to stay out of the Nicaraguan operation—because they might be needed for activities in their own country!

Costa Rica broke diplomatic relations with Cuba in September 1961, but this did not diminish the subversive activities. Recruiting for guerrilla training in Cuba was taken over by the Society of Friends of the Cuban Revolution (SARC). Later, with the help of the Cuban-trained guerrillas, a training course for 250 men was started in various parts of Costa Rica, including a farm owned by Marcial Eguiluz Orellana, Costa Rican left-wing politician. Later, Fidel Castro sent funds from Havana for Eguiluz to buy a radio station in Costa Rica.

Panama became a hotbed of Cuban-inspired Communist agitation. In August 1961, two Panamanian *Fidelistas,* Jaime Padilla Beliz and Guillermo Ríos Dugan, conferred with Ché Guevara in Havana. They were instructed to return to Panama, organize a *frente* of revolutionary factions including the powerful Vanguard of National Action (VAN) and the Panamanian Communist Party. Guevara supplied ample funds, and arranged for the Panamanians to ship needed supplies to Cuba and return to Panama with cargoes of arms and propaganda.

Young Communists and VAN members were sent to Cuba for training. During the summer of 1961, a privately owned ship, the *Alaska,* made several trips between Panama and Batabanó, on the southwestern coast of Cuba. On one trip it was loaded with lard, ball bearings, helicopter blades and three General Electric power plants worth $28,000. Three weeks later, the *Alaska* left Batabanó for Panama, carrying arms, propaganda material, and Panamanian graduates of the Minas del Frío school. The key man in this operation was a former Cubana Airlines pilot named Insua who reported to Sebastián Arcos, Cuban Undersecretary of Treasury.

Panama broke relations with Cuba in December 1961. But as recently as August 1962 armed bands of Cuban-trained guerrillas were operating in the mountains of Panama, duplicating the tactics which Fidel Castro had employed so successfully in the Sierra Maestra.

### *The Raid in Lima*

The actual operations of Castro Communists in Latin America via diplomatic channels were exposed in November 1960 as the result of a daring raid on the Cuban Embassy in Lima, Perú by a group of young anti-Communists headed by Frank Díaz Silveira.

Díaz Silveira, a 24-year-old Havana lawyer, joined the

anti-Castro underground early in 1960. After making several undercover trips between Miami and the Cuban hinterlands, he was assigned to represent the anti-Castro movement in Perú.

"After only two weeks in Lima," he says, "it was obvious that the nerve-center of subversive activities in Perú was the Cuban Embassy, then presided over by Ambassador Luis Ricardo Alonso Fernández. But what we needed was hard evidence. I drew up a plan and enlisted the aid of four trustworthy anti-Communists, one Cuban, one Chilean and two Argentines.

"On the afternoon of November 16, the young Argentine visited the embassy, which is on the sixth floor of an office building on Lima's *La Colmena,* and inquired about traveling in Cuba. While talking to the people there, he carefully surveyed the layout of the suites and the number of persons who worked in them. With this information we decided to raid the office late the next day.

"We were armed only with blackjacks, which we made from a long iron bar cut into four 12-inch sections and slipped into a rubber hose. We entered the building in two groups just before closing time, walking casually past the two Peruvian policemen on duty. On the sixth floor we tapped on the door which was opened by a receptionist. I told her quietly: 'This is a raid. If you don't resist or make an outcry, we will not harm you.' Then I locked the door and the boys moved swiftly through the rooms tearing out the telephones."

The few Cubans on duty at this late hour were terrified and offered no resistance. Díaz Silveira collared the ranking attaché and forced him to open the safe, and to produce the keys to the ambassador's locked desk. In one desk drawer he found a file marked Confidential; flipping through it he saw a list of labor organizations ("Organizaciones Sindicales") with large sums of money entered opposite the various names.

"We filled the one brief case we had brought with us," he says, "and then we picked up a large dispatch case and filled that. The boys meanwhile had tied up all employees and placed heavy adhesive tape over their mouths. We left in two groups, a few minutes apart, just as we had come in. We walked a few blocks, then hailed taxis which we changed three times before gathering at an apartment I had rented a week earlier. We worked all that night making copies of the documents on a copying machine I had ordered in Lima on a free-trial basis."

Quite aside from the amazing success of the raid and getaway, Díaz Silveira was blessed with another piece of luck. The Cuban Ambassador was winding up his affairs in Perú before taking a new assignment. On October 4 he had completed a report to the Ministry of Foreign Relations in Havana "giving an account of my work in defense of the Cuban revolution in Perú" and accounting for "funds delivered to the Peruvian Communist Party."

For example, in accounting for the disbursement of $30,000 received from Havana, Ambassador Alonso Fernández stated in his report that $15,000 had been allotted to party cells in various towns, listing the names of the Peruvians responsible. The balance had been paid to named newspapermen, labor leaders, Peruvian congressmen, and 34 politicians in eight different parties. Monthly payments ranged from $35 to $700.

"I am absolutely convinced," Alonso Fernández wrote, "that the work we are carrying out is the most effective possible, despite the constant surveillance I am under. . . . Perú must be considered the strategic center of the assault on capitalism, because of its geographic location, and the economic, political and social conflicts we can exploit." He added that the "technical advisors of the Soviet Union and the People's Republic of China have great hopes for the work we are doing in Perú.

"In accordance with instructions received from Commandante Raúl Castro, I have been occupying myself with the organization of insurrectional groups in connection with the Communist Party . . . as well as other friends of the Left . . . I am maintaining correspondence —not through the mails—with our ambassador in Quito [Ecuador] as well as the Ecuadorian ambassador in Lima. I am following instructions with regard to the tensions which exist between Perú and Ecuador because of the border problem . . . though I do not think it practical or convenient to make known here in Perú that our position is in favor of Ecuador, because we would then lose all that we have gained. . . ."

Díaz Silveira sent the original documents to Miami, then he mailed copies to important persons in the Peruvian Government. For several weeks the affair was hushed up while the Peruvian government conducted its own investigation. Then the sensational documents were disclosed in the Peruvian senate. On December 31, 1960, Perú severed diplomatic relations and gave the Cuban delegation 48 hours to get out of the country.

### *Evidence in Argentina*

Late one night in September 1961 Vitalio de la Torre, counsel of the Cuban Embassy in Buenos Aires, defected and took with him eighty-two documents from the embassy files. Again, Frank Díaz Silveira was a witness. "We were going to raid the embassy ourselves," Díaz Silveira says, "but this was not necessary when Vitalio was able to open up the files and take out the important papers. He was seventy-two years old, so the first thing we did was to get him safely out of the country before the storm broke. Otherwise, he surely would have been killed by the Argentine Communists."

The stolen documents created another international scandal. They revealed that Cuban Undersecretary of

State, Carlos Olivares Sánchez,* had sent to Guillermo Antich, chargé d'affaires in Buenos Aires, instructions to set up in Argentina secret guerrilla-training camps, conduct military espionage, promote sabotage, and foment unrest in labor unions and among university students. One document was even accompanied by detailed drawings showing how to make explosives and blow up bridges.

"Be cautious and discreet in everything," Olivares Sánchez warned, "and always adjust your ways in accordance with the instructions of Dr. Ernesto Guevara. . . . When verifying attacks in various places, always attribute them to Nazi-Fascist groups." In another communication, dated July 23, 1961, Olivares Sánchez wrote: "You know that while revolutions are always made from the outside, they nevertheless need a [national] base, so in this case you can serve us with exceptional usefulness." Antich also was instructed to do everything possible to create dissension among various Catholic organizations in Argentina so that they would fight among themselves instead of against Cuba.

Partly as a result of these disclosures, Antich was moved to Caracas, where he served as chargé d'affaires of the Cuban Embassy until he was declared *persona non grata* by the Venezuelan government. Nicolás Rivero has this to say about the man's unsavory record in the Cuban foreign service: "Antich was known in the Ministry as Raúl Castro's trusted man, and it was said that Raúl planted him there originally to spy on Foreign Minister Roberto Agramonte. As a matter of fact, Dr. Agramonte relieved Antich of his duties as a private secretary, because he delivered, without Agramonte's knowledge or consent, the Foreign Minister's private files into the hands of Castro's military intelligence."

Argentina broke diplomatic relations with Cuba in

* Appointed Cuban Ambassador to Russia on May 18, 1962.

February 1962, but the clandestine struggle continued. In April, following the severance of relations, Argentinians in Cuba organized a "Cuban-Argentine Friendship Institute," with headquarters in Havana and underground branches in Argentina. "The leading spirit in the Institute," a confidential report states, "is John William Cooke, who at one time was a chief of Perón's political machine. Cooke is still active in that faction of the Peronista party which works in concert with the Argentine Communists. Cooke maintains regular contact with these Peronistas and Communist sympathizers both inside and outside Argentina. One of his principal agents is his wife, Alicia Eguren de Cooke, a resident of Montevideo, Uruguay, who seems to have close liaison with people in Argentina. There is strong evidence that terrorist activities in Argentina by Peronista and Communist activists are financed and supplied from Havana via this channel."

On May 25, 1962, Ché Guevara addressed a rally in Havana to celebrate the Argentine national holiday, and expressed the hope that next year the Argentinians would be celebrating the occasion in their homeland "under the flag of socialism." At one point in his address, Ché declared: "Our revolution is one which needs to expand its ideas . . . and other people are helping us. Let the other people of the [Americas] get angry, take up arms, seize power, and aid us in this task which is the task of the entire hemisphere and of humanity."

### *Notes of a "Roving Ambassador"*

"There is scarcely a single country in Latin America which is not being infected with regular doses of Castro-communism," says Dr. José Ignacio Rasco, who has traveled extensively throughout Central and South America since early 1961 as an observer and "roving ambassador" for the Cuban Revolutionary Council and the Democratic

Christian Movement. Dr. Rasco supplies the following notes (quoted with permission) from his confidential reports:

*Brazil:* "This is one of the main targets and a country in far more danger of Communist takeover than many believe. Over the last two years Cuban agents have kept in close touch with Francisco Julião, the admitted Marxist who heads the Peasant Leagues in poverty-ridden northeast Brazil. Flights directly from this region to Cuba have been set up by Cubana Airlines, and there is no doubt that Julião has been financed from Havana. The Leagues have received arms from Cuba. The prospect of a civil war in Brazil is one reason why Julião sent his family to Cuba, according to Communist leaders in Brazil.

"Julião has traveled to Cuba, and there have been visits by members of the Peasant Leagues who purportedly took agricultural courses. They returned to Brazil far more knowledgeable in ideological indoctrination.

"Brazil is an excellent example of a disturbing development that I have found throughout Latin America. It is this: The intellectuals and pseudo-intellectuals who often have a powerful impact on opinion, especially in some of the governmental circles, have taken far longer to understand how Cuba has been deceived by the Communists than has the common man. All too often the intelligentsia has been the last to face up to reality. They have been the most stubborn in refusing to believe the facts about the suffering of the Cubans, not only the terrible shortages of food, but the imprisonment, atrocities and executions.

"These are things, however, that have gotten through to most of the common people in Latin America despite the fact that Cuban Communist propaganda spends five dollars to every one dollar spent for anti-Castro propaganda. Yet this propaganda cannot counter three shocking facts: at least 4,000 Cubans have been shot at the *paredón,* 100,000 political prisoners are in Castro's jails and

300,000 Cubans have left their homeland. This is why public opinion in Latin America has gone through four stages in its attitude toward Castro: (1) adulation; (2) confusion; (3) doubt; and (4) repudiation.

"This is why the Cuban Communists have resorted more and more to subversion, espionage and a barrage of propaganda inciting revolt. When a Brazilian Communist conferred with Fidel Castro last May [1962], the Brazilian later reported that Castro was unhappy with the Brazilian Communist Party because it had failed 'to take a strong revolutionary line' in accordance with the edict of the 22nd Party Congress of the Communist Party of the Soviet Union. Fidel said he was behind this tactic and pressed the Brazilians to get on with guerrilla activities 'as soon as possible.'"

*Chile:* "Here is another danger spot that in the months ahead may well be the next great 'crisis area.' Senator Salvador Allende, who heads Chile's Communist-dominated popular front, is a presidential candidate who actually stands a good chance of being elected. He has visited Cuba twice and is reported to have close personal ties with many Castro officials.

"Chile is one of the five Latin-American countries that still [December 1962] maintain diplomatic relations with Cuba. The others are Brazil, Uruguay, Bolivia and Mexico. This has left the door open for subversion. For example, a clandestine printing press in the home of Julio Bocanegra, who also prints propaganda for the Chilean Communist Party, turns out Cuban propaganda under the direction of Orlando Prendes, cultural attaché at the Cuban Embassy."

*Bolivia:* "This is a hotbed of Cuban Communist conspiracy. The Cuban ambassador was ordered to leave the country in 1960 for interfering in Bolivia's internal affairs. When documents were released by the Bolivian government in June 1961 showing a Red plot to take over the government, one of them contained evidence that the Cuban Embassy had distributed funds to several Bolivians. As a result, the Cuban chargé García Triana was also requested to leave Bolivia."

*Ecuador:* "Here a pro-Castro Revolutionary Union of Ecuadorian Youth (URJE) has not only received $22,000 from the Cuban government but its leader and other members were given guerrilla training in Cuba. The URJE played a major role in a two-day riot in April 1962."

*Uruguay:* "The Cuban Embassy in Uruguay is a center for subversion, and in January 1961 the Cuban ambassador was told to leave Uruguay because of his intervention. His name is Mario García Incháustegui, the same man who became Cuba's representative at the U.N. and the one who so vociferously denied the presence of missiles in Cuba and attacked the U.S. when it imposed its blockade. He was then recalled to Havana and replaced by Carlos Lechuga."

*Guatemala:* "A new Communist guerrilla front known as the November 13 Group was set up in March 1962 by a Cuban agent and supported with $10,000. This money was handed over to its leader in Mexico with word from Castro that more would be forthcoming if the group was successful. When the orthodox Communist Party representatives complained about not being given this money, they were told that Castro was displeased by their unwillingness to fight the Guatemalan government. The Cuban emissary said: 'It is not a matter of standing around with Arab fatalism waiting for events to take place. We should act efficiently so as to precipitate the death of imperialism. Because of this we are ready to help anyone who may decide to struggle against imperialism anywhere.'

"Despite this and much more," says José Ignacio Rasco, "there is still a dangerous blindness by many persons in Latin America who should know better by now. I have heard the same arguments that were used in Cuba to demonstrate that 'communism can't happen here' repeated in country after country. For example, they say communism can't take over because the army is anti-communist, because there is a very strong middle class, because there are foreign investments in the country, because the people are very Catholic, and because the Communists are only a few. They say that there is no hatred in their countries, there are no great rifts in the classes. Yet in Cuba we had every one of those conditions, even to a more favorable degree."

### *The Camilo Plan*

Venezuela, fed up with Cuban interference in its internal affairs, broke off relations in November 1961. Nevertheless, terrorist activity aimed at the overthrow of the government continued. The Central University in Caracas remained a hot-bed of Communist operations where professional agitators, trained in Cuba, recruited and armed Venezuelan activists and saboteurs. "The university has served as an arsenal," the newspaper *El Universal* reported, "literally many small fortresses [which] supply those fighting the democratic system." Guerrilla bands operated in the mountains of western Venezuela with arms smuggled in from Cuba; although many of the guerrillas were killed or captured by government troops, the elusive bands managed to carry on, much as did Castro's rebels in the Sierra Maestra during the years 1957–1958 while vastly outnumbered by well-armed Batista troops. But, in Venezuela, the primary target was the rich, vast oil fields, source of much of the hemisphere's power, and a prize envied by Fidel Castro's fuel-starved economy.

On the night of October 27, 1962, four men later identified as Pedro Díaz Sifontes, Rafael Colmenares, Tulio Ramón Peña Escalona, and Eulogio del Moral, all members of the Venezuelan Communist Party, put out in a small boat from Puerto Alegre on the shores of Lake Maracaibo. Their mission was to blow up four of the key power substations of the Creole petroleum company situated in the oil-rich lake facing the Tía Juana coast.

The explosives they carried were dynamite cartridges packed, with their fuses, inside cardboard milk containers. The detonator of the bombs was an ingenious although simple device typical of most handbooks on sabotage and guerrilla warfare. Black acid was poured into a wide-mouthed bottle which was then stoppered with rolled newspaper, and the inverted bottle was placed atop the dynamite-loaded milk carton. When the acid burned through the wadded paper the fuse was ignited, producing both intense flames and a powerful explosion.

At 8:30 that night, the four men reached the first substation, designated as No. 37. One man remained in the boat to prepare and pass the explosives; the other three boarded the substation and placed the bombs in strategic spots. Four charges were placed aboard the first substation; three each aboard the second and third; and the remaining two were arranged on the fourth platform.

However, as the boat was pulling away from the fourth and last substation, del Moral heard a sound "like a skyrocket when its fuse is lit." This was followed by an explosion which blasted all four men into the air. Díaz Sifontes managed to swim ashore and then disappeared; Eulogio del Moral reached an electrical tower in the lake, climbed aboard, and then hauled up Tulio Peña, whose hands were so badly burned that he could not help himself. Only Colmenares was unaccounted for.

Three hours later, del Moral and Tulio Peña were taken from the tower by officers of the Police Administration and placed under arrest. Both made full confessions which disclosed the details of the conspiracy and its Cuban origin. The operation, they revealed, was only one isolated phase of the "Camilo Plan," named in honor of the late "hero of the revolution," Camilo Cienfuegos, who had vanished mysteriously during the Hubert Matos affair.

According to Señor Nelson Himiob, Interim Representative of Venezuela to the Organization of American States, who presented the documentary evidence to the OAS Council on November 8, 1962, the Venezuelan Police Administration already had picked up information indicating that some such operation was under way. "On Wednesday, the 24th of October," he reported, "an unidentified ship, sailing northwest of Curaçao, transmitted instructions, emanating from Havana, that 'the moment had arrived to carry out the Camilo Plan.' The Police Administration at Maracaibo also had information that [the Camilo Plan] was to be an action of importance that would begin with isolated explosions in the oil fields."

A few hours after the explosions, two Communists were arrested in a town near Maracaibo while celebrating the success of the operation. "They said that Pedro Díaz Sifontes had triumphed," Señor Himiob told the OAS, "for which he would be given a great reception when he reached Havana. If Díaz Sifontes were to reach Havana the Cuban government undoubtedly would receive him with great honors. If we had any doubts about that they would be dispelled by one paragraph in a speech made by Raúl Castro in Santiago de Cuba on October 29th, in which he enthusiastically reported events in various Latin American countries, among them the sabotage in my country's petroleum zone."

These were Raúl Castro's words: "At the very time of delivery of [President John F.] Kennedy's aggressive speech which provoked this grave international crisis, in the streets of Santiago, Chile, a demonstration of support of Castro was being carried on. In Bolivia a demonstration of support of the Cuban revolution was attacked by fascist bands armed by the North American Embassy, causing the death of five workers. In Venezuela groups of revolutionary guerrillas blew up four electric plants belonging to imperialistic petroleum-exploiting companies. And thus, successively, one after another, all the countries of this continent, our brother peoples, in defenseless but combative demonstrations in the streets of all its cities, have demonstrated their determined support of the cause of the Cuban revolution."

Señor Himiob then produced a radiogram, addressed to a Communist group at the university in Caracas, and intercepted by the Venezuela government on October 27, 1962:

"Increased movement of North American troops in the Caribbean area and obstinate Kennedy attitude indicates imminence of imperialistic attack against our fatherland. We request redoubling of immediate, effective, concrete actions against imperialist aggressors in front of North American embassies and consulates in every country. Cuba will resist and repulse imperialistic attack. Fatherland or death!"

Says Señor Himiob: "This was signed by the FEU, CUBA, which corresponds to the Federation of University Students of Cuba. The message was dispatched in plain language, not code; and this seems to indicate the intention of the sender that the Venezuelan Government, or other governments that might receive it, might publish it as proof of Castro's instigation of subversive movements. The Cuban government might then have dismissed it scornfully as a 'student matter.' But in view of the interventionist record of Castroism, it is unquestionable that the objective was connected with acts of subversion and terrorism."

On the night of the sabotage in Lake Maracaibo, President Betancourt of Venezuela declared: "Even before there was evidence that Cuba had been converted into a base for powerful missiles, placed there by the Soviet

Union, the Venezuelan government already had pointed out the dangers of a regime which exported passwords, money and arms for the purpose of sapping and destroying regimes of pure democratic origin firmly opposed to converting themselves into submissive appendages of Moscow."

### *The Voice of Fidelismo*

On May Day, 1961, Fidel Castro proudly inaugurated Radio Havana Cuba which, he had promised, would bring his "truths to the four corners of the world." This was no exaggeration. The $35 million installation of Swiss and Czech equipment gave him five 100,000-watt transmitters, the most powerful in Latin America. Immediately, they began to bombard Central and South America with 106 hours a week of propaganda in Spanish, Portuguese, French, English and even the Quechua dialect spoken by fourteen million Indians in the Andes. Fidel Castro was making good his boast: "Our small fatherland today represents interests which go far beyond our borders. . . . We have been given a glorious destiny. We will be a light which will become more brilliant, and its rays will extend farther each day over the lands of fraternal Latin America."

Special weekly programs are beamed at Perú, Honduras, Nicaragua, Guatemala, the Dominican Republic. At seven o'clock on Sunday evenings, the Peruvian Anti-Imperialist Struggle Movement, based in Havana, goes on the air. On Mondays and Thursdays the Nicaraguan Unity Front broadcasts the "Voice of the Nicaraguan Revolution." The former left-wing president of Guatemala, Jacobo Arbenz, now a resident of Havana, broadcasts the Red line to his homeland on Tuesdays and Saturdays.

On April 23, 1962, for example, the "Voice of Revolutionary Perú" declared: "We would like to read the manifesto which Peruvian students, who are here in this free territory of the Americas on scholarships granted by the Cuban revolutionary government, have placed in our hands. It says: 'Latin America is going through a time of decision. The nations are rising against their oppressors, and in this struggle which they are waging for their national liberation, Cuba is in the vanguard of the Latin American Revolution.' "

On May 5, 1962, the "Dominican Liberation Movement," based in Havana, broadcast: "All revolutionary Dominicans must support this movement of popular revolt and help it constantly to perfect and attain its combat objectives."

On June 12, the "Revolutionary Voice of Perú" sounded the call to rebellion: "The transformation of Perú is the collective task of the workers, peasants, intellectuals, men and women of Perú who have the revolutionary faith to liquidate the archaic economic, political and social system of our country." On August 28, the tone was even more inflammatory: "In these hours when the danger of Yankee aggression hangs over the Cuban revolution, the Peruvian people must respond throughout the country. In the universities, mountain communities, cities, places of work and wherever else imperialism and oligarchy exercise their exploitation, the people of Perú must respond by demonstrating their support of Cuba, and their violent objection to serving as U.S. slaves."

Actually, this was the voice of Moscow speaking from Havana. For the union between the Kremlin and Cuba by now was sealed with the bonds of 55 diplomatic commitments, protocols, agreements and treaties. No longer was even the flimsiest attempt made to hide the fact of Soviet power behind the Cuban offensive in Latin America.

Cuba's Communist Party chieftain, Blas Roca, turned up in Montevideo in June 1962, in the company of leading

Communists from Europe and Latin America, to address the 18th annual congress of the Uruguayan Communist Party. "Throughout the world," he said, "the Cuban revolution represents the historic confirmation of the thesis stated in the Declaration of the 81 Communist Parties and in the program of the Communist Party of the Soviet Union. This is the period of transition from capitalism to socialism. Cuba has initiated the triumph of socialism on our continent."

Ché Guevara, high priest of Latin American communism, had preached the same gospel, but more explicitly, on April 30. "The continent lives in a state of turmoil," said Ché. "The popular masses await the moment to join the struggle. But we [Cubans] have been entrusted with the enormous responsibility of being in the vanguard. We must think of the tragic realities of America today—people hoping to achieve power by whatever means possible, and the imperialistic exploiters ready to stop, with blood and fire, the popular movement.

"In Guatemala, the guerrillas dominate many parts of the country, and students and workers are chasing the forces of repression from the capital.

"In Venezuela popular forces are fighting in every corner of the country and getting stronger and more daring in what once appeared to be a solid bastion of imperialism.

"In Colombia the forces of the people struggle and organize again and again, despite the many heroes who have paid with their lives for daring to oppose the two oligarchic castes which, every four years, dispute as to which side will snatch power from the other.

"Subterranean rumblings are heard all over the world. In Latin America a volcano is erupting—a volcano of which imperialism, despite its deaf ears, despite its contempt for the people, despite its false sense of superiority, is well aware!"

# Part Seven

# THE KREMLIN-WEST

Toward the end of 1961, Fidel Castro decided that the time had come to end the masquerade and appear before Cuba and the world in his true color—red. Instead of dealing in innuendo, flirting coyly with Marxist-Leninist terminology, he began to speak out boldly, even imprudently. For example, in November, when he lectured the first congress of "revolutionary orientators" on their unique role in the new society, he still advocated the cautious approach.

"In Cuba," he said, "the commissar is never a commissar, he is a 'revolutionary instructor'—although we must admit that commissar is a good word. The former agitator and propagandist is not a propagandist or agitator . . . because those words belong more to the period of struggle for power when it was necessary to agitate. There are other times when it is necessary to awaken the revolutionary spirit. Then it is right and, above all, it is necessary to *orientate.*

"The word 'indoctrinate' is not good. What impression does it give? It implies that you are putting something into the head of an individual by simply repeating things, as if the individual has nothing in his head and that you are stuffing it into him. When you try to stuff ideas into their heads people will say, 'They will not indoctrinate me!'

"The 'revolutionary instructor' is the term to be substituted for 'indoctrinator.' The 'orientator' is the substitute for 'agitator,' although it means the same thing. Imagine what would happen if we called this organization [Commission for Revolutionary Orientation] the 'National Commission for Revolutionary Agitation!' These are words which have infuriated our enemies. Therefore, new words must be substituted. . . ."

Then, on the night of December 2, in a five-hour telecast announcing the formation of a Soviet-style "united party of the Cuban socialist revolution," he decided to abandon cautious terminology and call a Communist spade a spade.

"I am a Marxist-Leninist," he asserted proudly, "and I will be a Marxist-Leninist to the last day of my life!"

He went further: "Now, then, do I believe in Marxism? I absolutely believe in Marxism! Did I believe in Marxism on the first of January [1959]? I did believe on the first of January! Did I believe on the 26th of July [1953]? I did believe on the 26th of July!

"Do I have any doubts about Marxism? Do I think some interpretations are erroneous and should be revised? I have not the least doubt! Quite the contrary is true in my case. . . . And how am I a Marxist-Leninist? Halfway? We revolutionaries do not know how to do anything halfway! We only know how to do things one hundred per cent!"

### *The Castro Confession*

Castro proceeded to confess, in true Communist fashion, the "errors" in his early political thinking. "There was a time when, politically, I could consider myself illiterate, wholly illiterate, as a result of my class origin," he said. "Twenty years ago, did I know more about revolution than Juan Marinello, Carlos Rafael Rodríguez, Aníbal Escalante, Blas Roca? No, gentlemen!

"During my first days in the university, I began to conceive some revolutionary ideas while studying bourgeois political economy. Later, of course, we began making our first contacts with the *Communist Manifesto*, with the works of Marx, Engels, Lenin and all that. That marked the first stage.

"When we left the university, in my own case, I had been greatly influenced. I will not say I was Marxist-Leninist by a long shot. I may have had two million petty bourgeois prejudices and a whole string of ideas which I am glad I do not hold today. In sum, certain circumstances were favorable. Our revolutionary thinking was strongly influenced by contact, and that is how things got started. . . ."

A few weeks later, on December 22, while addressing the graduating class of the "revolutionary instruction school" for militiamen, Fidel Castro unveiled his reasons for having deceived the Cuban people with assurances that "the revolution is not red but olive-green." By concealing the true nature and objectives of the revolution, he said, "we acted in the Marxist-Leninist manner. . . . If we had paused to tell the people, 'We are Marxist-Leninist,' while we were on the Pico Turquino [in the Sierra Maestra] and not yet strong, it is possible that we never would have been able to descend to the plains."

"There were signs," says Dr. Jorge Castellanos, "that the Communist hierarchy in Moscow and Havana considered Castro's 'confession' imprudent and premature. Despite the fact that Castro's December 2 speech had been televised, the portions dealing with his avowed Communist past were omitted from the version published in *Revolución*. In Moscow, *Pravda* ignored the speech, and only many days later did other Soviet papers publish the Tass news agency report from Havana which acclaimed Castro as a 'new Marxist-Leninist.' "

Castro's confession had a terrific impact on Cubans everywhere; but to the beaten, depressed, hungry people within Cuba the words cut like another whiplash. They had only to look around them to see what Castro's Marxism had done to their country and to their lives.

INRA, the super-state created in the guise of agrarian reform, had wrecked the Cuban economy and reduced living standards to levels prevailing in Eastern Europe and Red China. Agricultural production in virtually all crops had fallen far below pre-1959 records. The traditionally abundant sugar crop was so short in 1961 that Castro's Cuba was unable to meet even its commitments to the Soviet Union. In April 1962, Alfredo Menéndez, production commissar of the sugar industry, in a confidential report to Minister of Industry, Ché Guevara, broke the bad news that the 1962 *zafra* (cane crop) would be smaller still.

Citing the production shortages of the cane cooperatives and "communal farms," Menéndez reported: "Everyone is well aware of the disorganization of these two sectors, and their loss of conscience regarding the need to produce cane, owing to the policy carried out by the Agrarian Reform Institute (INRA). In these two sectors, cane cooperatives and communal farms, there is total disorganization and apathy with respect to cane production, and this is sharply reflected in the present harvest."

Regarding the cane growers who were still outside the collectives and cooperatives, and who had not yet been drawn into the regime's "Small Farmers' Association," Menéndez stated: "This sector is completely disoriented politically. In some cases, they have abandoned their production units; in some, they have adopted an openly counter-revolutionary attitude; and in others they are intimidated by the arbitrary, improper measures taken by irresponsible officials."

Consumer goods of all types vanished from the Cuban markets. After two years of shortages, stringent rationing of foodstuffs began early in 1962. Clothing, shoes, drugs, cosmetics, even toothpaste and toothbrushes were unobtainable. Soap of inferior quality was rationed at one small cake per person each month; Fidel Castro declared solemnly: "That should suffice if used carefully." Meat and poultry, once so plentiful in Cuba, were unobtainable even in the small amounts specified by the ration cards. Staples like rice, sweet potatoes and the common *malanga* root became scarce. Cubans called their common black beans "Dr. Castro's little pills with Vitamin G-2 added."

Yet somehow the hard-pressed Cubans kept the remarkable sense of humor which is a national characteristic. Most of their bitter jests, unfortunately, involve puns and plays on words in Spanish that are untranslatable. However, one story, popular in the spring of 1962, transcends the language barrier to provide a sardonic comment on life in Castro's Cuba.

A Cuban died ("with great relief") and went to Heaven where St. Peter greeted him with the news that, because of the life he had led, he would have to spend an eternity in Hell. "However," St. Peter added, "things have changed somewhat. We now have, in addition to the old capitalist hell, a new Communist hell. Look them over, and take your choice."

The Cuban visited the capitalist hell, where the devil-in-charge showed him around and explained the variety of tortures available—lighted matches shoved under the fingernails, burning cigarettes pressed against the eyeballs, immersion in boiling oil. With a shudder the visitor excused himself by saying that he would look around before making up his mind. Whereupon he went to the Communist hell. It was more modern, more efficient, but the torments described by the Infernal Escort—lighted matches, burning cigarettes, boiling oil—were exactly the same.

"Forgive me for wasting your time," the Cuban said. "But I think I would prefer the Old Hell—most of my friends are there."

Then, as he turned to leave, he heard a hushed voice from somewhere in the sulphurous depths: "Chico, don't be a fool—stay where you are! In this Communist hell *they have no matches, no cigarettes, no oil to boil!*"

### *The Bitter Fruit*

Cubans were not starving, but daily they felt the gnawing, humiliating hunger-pangs of deprivation which can make a proud people fighting mad. Worse than physical hunger, however, was the awareness of lost freedom and spiritual values. Prisons were jampacked with nearly 100,000 Cubans whose only crime was opposition to Castro and Communism. The only security lay in silence or assent. To openly dissent or doubt meant to invite the mark of "counter-revolutionary," and counter-revolutionaries went into jails or to the *paredón*. The sounds of the firing squads were daily reminders to those outside the prison walls that some prisoners were finding, at least, the ultimate release in death.

In a nation that always took pride in family unity, tragically broken families had become commonplace. Children denounced parents to *vigilantes* and the political police. Wives went into exile alone, leaving behind husbands who had become devout *fidelistas* or converts to communism. Children too were left behind, sometimes at the insistence of one parent, but often because the child or teen-ager had succumbed completely to the Castro mesmerism.

"Cuba's disillusionment was painfully complete," says "Padre Humberto," the Protestant minister who laid aside his cloth to fight in the anti-Castro underground. "The so-called 'little people' to whom Fidel Castro had dedicated the revolution could be fooled no longer. The angry *campesinos* were not only refusing to cut the cane but now were burning the canefields. Disillusioned workers were sabotaging machinery and throwing away their tools. Sabotage was increasing everywhere despite the greater number of militiamen who guarded the factories and fields, because the disgruntled *milicianos* usually closed their eyes or looked the other way. And often the saboteurs were the *milicianos* themselves.

"Except for the kids, who were too young to remember, every Cuban knew that Castro and his spokesmen were lying when they described pre-1959 Cuba as an underdeveloped country with a low standard of living and a poverty-ridden population. What little we had under Castro only served to remind us of how good things had been before. Yes, Cuba was politically immature and, under Batista, even politically corrupt. And, like most advanced nations, we had some economic and social sore-spots that needed to be changed. But, in the years before 1959, we had made tremendous economic and social advances. We had achieved a living standard that was among the highest in the Americas and, perhaps, in the world. What shortcomings we had were largely in the political area and these, along with our lesser economic and social problems, could have been overcome (as Castro hoodwinked us into believing they would be) within the democratic framework of the 1940 Constitution and without any recourse to Marxism."

Castro and his Communist and left-wing apologists have not only presented a distorted image of pre-1959 Cuba, but they also have consistently denounced as "imperialist" and "counter-revolutionary" propaganda every statement to the contrary. However, Aníbal Escalante, who was at the time a most respected member of the Cuban Communist hierarchy, stated the facts plainly in *Verde Olivo*, the widely circulated magazine of the Cuban armed forces, in July 1961. And, in doing so, he rubbed salt into raw Cuban wounds.

Escalante, with a voice pitched to the other Americas, was preaching the new gospel that a nation need not be economically backward or socially depressed in order to be ripe for communism.

"In effect," he wrote, "Cuba was not one of the countries with the lowest standard of living for the masses in America. On the contrary, [Cuba] had one of the highest standards of living. Yet it was here that the first great democratic, socialistic and patriotic revolution of the continent broke out. . . . If historical development had been governed by the false axiom [that poverty and backwardness are prerequisites of communism], the revolution should have occurred first in Haiti, Bolivia, Colombia, or even Chile, countries of much greater poverty than Cuba in 1952 or 1958."

### *Operation Cuba: Phase One*

"The Soviet military buildup of Cuba," says Fernandez Cavada of the Unidad Revolucionaria, "began after the Mikoyan visit to Havana in February 1960, which resulted in Raúl Castro's trip to Moscow and Prague. The purpose of Raúl's mission, as is now well known, was to seek Soviet armaments and, if possible, to have Cuba admitted to the Warsaw Pact. He apparently failed in the latter, but not long after he returned to Cuba, the first Russian and Czech military equipment began to arrive."

Alonso Quintero, stevedore and later an expert crane operator on docks in the Havana area, witnessed the arrival of the Soviet ships in the spring of 1961. "There was great public interest in 'Russian aid,'" he says. "People were under the impression that the ships would bring food and many of the things which were in short supply. But I was in a position to see that few of the cargoes consisted of food and merchandise. On the rare occasions when they did, there was much publicity. But otherwise the docks were closed. We were not permitted to leave until the ships had been completely unloaded. We slept on the docks, worked in shifts, and our food was provided. The area was heavily guarded by the militia and there were always a few Russian officials, who were treated with great deference by the Cuban army officers, on hand to supervise the unloading.

"Aside from the crated material, which we assumed to be rifles and ammunition, I helped to unload tanks, trucks, jeeps, multi-barreled anti-aircraft guns, heavy artillery and what I was able to identify as the fuselages of fighter aircraft. During the early days we were often paid a bonus of $100 in addition to a week's salary and told to keep our mouths shut about what we saw. Trustworthy crane operators were at a premium. Some men refused to work and gave as an excuse that they were afraid to handle stuff that might blow up. But I remember five or six instances in which the operators 'accidentally' tipped the platform and sent crates crashing onto the docks or even managed to drop cannons or tanks into the water. That kind of sabotage did not go on for long, however, because in every case the worker was arrested and sent away for a long prison term. I quit my job shortly before the invasion and after that I fished for a living."

Ramón Valdivia, a former lawyer, was imprisoned as a suspected counter-revolutionary in April 1961; when he was released in October the first thing he noticed was the presence in Havana of many more Russians, Czechs, Poles and Chinese. "They kept very much to themselves," he says, "but they stood out very conspicuously in any Cuban crowd or community. The Russians and Czechs had taken over some of the finest mansions in the Vedado district. They had their own commissaries, which were well stocked with provisions that were scarce or unobtainable on the local market. Many had brought their wives and families, and there was even a private school, staffed with Russian teachers, for the children of the high-ranking Soviet officers.

"These people were supposed to be industrial and agricultural technicians, and members of various trade missions, which became the subject of much joking among Cubans. Perhaps some of them were civilians, but the majority were military specialists. I was in Vienna for a time after World War II when the city was partly occupied by the Soviets, and I can spot a Russian officer even when he is dressed in civilian clothes."

Oscar Sardiñas, formerly a sugar mill engineer, encountered a group of forty "agricultural technicians" from the Soviet Union who came to inspect the Camilo Cienfuegos cooperative in Matanzas during the summer of 1961. "There were about ten in the party who spoke Spanish quite well and I got to know them," Sardiñas says. "One night, at a party where there was much drinking, several of them said enough to disclose to us that they were graduates of military academies. There was one fellow who got quite drunk and cursed his luck in being sent to Cuba; he had been angling for an embassy post elsewhere in Latin America, and obviously not as an 'agricultural technician.' We, of course, confined our conversation to agriculture and asked only the most innocent questions about various aspects of farming in the Soviet Union. It was quite obvious that the Russians didn't know what we were talking about. They were military men and knew little else."

During 1960–1961, and with quickened pace following the abortive invasion of the Bay of Pigs, Soviet arms poured into Cuba to secure the Castro regime against "aggression" as well as internal uprisings. The rebel army was whittled down to a hard core of dependable officers and men. The civilian militia was expanded into a vast "national guard" numbering approximately 300,000 men plus a women's auxiliary of well trained and somewhat fanatic amazons. From the ranks of the *milicianos,* the brightest, sturdiest, and most politically reliable boys were invited to try out for the *Cinco Picos,* so-called for having survived rugged training which involved climbing the Pico Turquino in the Sierra Maestra at least five times. The *Cinco Picos* (an estimated 40,000 men) became the elite corps of the Cuban army.

U.S.-Cuban intelligence sources estimated that during 1960–1961 Castro acquired from the Sino-Soviet bloc between 150 and 250 heavy tanks, up to 100 assault guns, between 500 and 1,000 pieces of field artillery, possibly 1,000 anti-aircraft batteries, several hundred thousand automatic rifles and small arms, and a number of patrol vessels and torpedo boats. He had received between 50 and 75 MIG fighters, many of which were still crated and awaiting the arrival of the 200 or more Cuban pilots who were being trained behind the Iron Curtain.

Thus, by the end of 1961, Castro's armed forces had been transformed from a band of bearded guerrillas and armed schoolboys into a tightly knit, disciplined modern army equipped with modern weapons and trained under the firm command of Sino-Soviet military technicians.

### *The Big Parade*

Cubans, as well as some foreign observers, got a partial but impressive glimpse of Castro's new military power on January 2, 1962, the third anniversary of the revolution. Havana's Plaza de la Revolución was transformed into a tropical Red Square for the occasion. The historic monument of José Martí, backed by towering portraits of Fidel Castro and Lenin, became a sort of "Lenin's Tomb" from which Castro, his Cuban commissars and a covey of Sino-Soviet guests, watched the big parade. For nearly two hours half a million Cubans jammed the plaza while army, militia, naval units, and labor battalions passed in review. This time the high point of the celebration was not Fidel Castro's loud, arrogant, vituperative oratory, but what to

Cuban eyes was a dazzling display of Soviet arms—artillery equipped with radar devices, multiple-barrel anti-aircraft guns, mobile rocket launchers, heavy artillery and fifty-ton tanks. Soviet MIG-17s and MIG-19s flown, presumably, by Cuban pilots trained in the Soviet Union, zoomed overhead in tight formations.

"Yes, we Habañeros went home that night with plenty to think about," says Ramón Valdivia. "Fidel and his Soviet comrades had put on an impressive show. One had to admit, however grudgingly, that any future invasion of Cuba would meet counter-measures that would make the Bay of Pigs look like a Boy Scout maneuver.

"But we also had some good questions to ask. For instance, in any war of liberation, how many of these well-armed soldiers and *milicianos* would turn their weapons against the Cuban liberators and their allies? How many would lay down their arms or go over to the other side? In early 1962, the Cuban consensus was that, except for the elite corps, the Communists, and the young hot-heads in the militia, the majority of Cubans whom Fidel Castro had under arms would be among the first to turn and strike the blow for freedom."

"Popular unrest was seething in Cuba during early 1962," says Padre Humberto. "It seemed about to erupt violently in late spring. Not only was sabotage on the rise, and absenteeism (which the regime condemned as 'the most vicious form of sabotage') spreading in the factories and on farms, but the activities of our guerrillas in the hills and mountains were getting to be more than Castro, with all his modern arms, could cope with. The wide-open civic resistance, exemplified by the so-called 'hunger marches' and public demonstrations which began in June, was much more serious than the outside world realized.

"People outside Cuba, even some Cubans in exile, I regret to say, discounted these sporadic events as feeble, futile efforts which were no more effective than pin pricks, perhaps, against the firmly entrenched and well-armed regime. Yet none was feeble or futile; even the smallest evidence of popular protest fanned the flame of the Cuban will-to-resist and kept the fires of revolt burning.

"Fidel Castro never made the mistake of deprecating these manifestations as did some of our friends. Castro was haunted by the awareness that, under his leadership, a mere handful of rebels, supported by an angry people, had been able to overthrow the powerful Batista regime. He had seen resentment, disillusionment, lack of faith demoralize Batista's big army until the dictator feared that his own men might turn their guns against him. Fidel could see the same kind of force mounting up to crush him in the demoralization of the militia and the open defiance being manifested increasingly by the Cuban masses. That is why the government decided to make a 'show of force' by sending tanks and artillery against the people of Cárdenas [100 miles east of Havana] and even sending President Dorticós to the 'revolutionary mass meeting' which was staged as a counter-demonstration."

### *What Happened in Cárdenas*

The Cárdenas affair, which reached a climax about noontime on June 16, 1962, was not an isolated incident; similar popular uprisings occurred both before and after that date in a number of towns and cities—Matanzas, Jovellanos, Limonar, El Cano and elsewhere. But Fidel Castro chose Cárdenas, a city with a population of 55,000, as the example to convince Cubans that the regime would not tolerate opposition but would stamp out, by force of arms if necessary, any manifestation of popular unrest.

There have been many accounts of what happened in Cárdenas that day; the following is taken from a letter written by an unusually trustworthy eyewitness:

"For many weeks, even months, there had been much

grumbling and some noisy protests among the housewives who queued up in front of the various shops and markets with their ration cards, waiting to buy food that was in short supply or never to be had. At first this was tempered by jokes and laughter, like taunting the militiamen and making loud remarks about the well-fed Russians and Poles and the fat Chinese. But by mid-June there was less laughter; tempers were getting short, there were more arguments, fights and outcries.

"On this Saturday morning [June 16] the downtown area of Cárdenas was crowded with as many men—farmers, factory laborers, dock workers—as women. The trouble started, innocently enough, with a peaceful procession of women. I saw them coming down the wide street toward the Parque de Colón. Most of them carried pots, pans and other cooking utensils as symbols of their status as housewives, and all carried their 'deceivers' [ration cards] which they waved in the air. Their destination was the town hall, where they planned to register a peaceful protest against the food shortage and, after that, to assemble for prayers in the Church of the Purísima Concepción.

"However, as the procession passed the markets surrounding the Plaza del Mercado, many people deserted the long food lines and joined the marchers. Some of the women began beating pots and pans, and the others took up the beat in unison. Then the chanting began: 'We are hungry!' 'Fidel we want food!' 'Cuba, Sí! Comunismo, no!' Soon the cries got bolder: 'Down with communism!' 'Down with Castro!'

"The commotion drew crowds from the side streets, and before long the housewives' procession was lost in the mob. The streets were jammed for blocks around. When police and militiamen tried to halt the mob at crossings they were practically trampled underfoot. They couldn't possibly break up or control the crowds.

"Groups of Communist thugs recruited from the dock workers' union came to the assistance of the police and the fighting started. At one point, a huge army truck equipped with a loud-speaker tried to plow through the mass of people. The voice over the loudspeaker was saying: 'Food is coming. . . . Fidel has said that food is on the way. . . . *Patria o Muerte! Venceremos!* [Fatherland or Death! We will win!]' The mob stopped the truck, beat up the driver, and made the other fellow shout over the loud-speaker 'Down with communism!'

"The rioting went on for hours. But word must have been flashed to Havana very early, because by afternoon the troops began to arrive. These were Unit 20-28 of the Revolutionary Army and three battalions from Division 14-10 which was garrisoned in Matanzas. The roads leading into Cárdenas were lined with Soviet tanks, weapon carriers, field artillery, anti-aircraft guns and truckload after truckload of armed soldiers. Two Soviet 'Kronstadt' sub-chasers appeared in the harbor with deck-guns manned and ready for action. A formation of MIG fighters flew back and forth over the city for the rest of the day.

"President Dorticós arrived with the troops from Havana. A rostrum was set up in the Explanada in front of the museum-library and behind it they set up an enormous sign reading 'Socialism is Peace.' It was truly amazing how thoroughly this 'revolutionary mass meeting' was organized in such a short time."

## *"Little Budapest"*

Television carried nearly every aspect of the Cárdenas uprising throughout Cuba—the mob scenes, the military show-of-force, and finally the long, impassioned speech by Dorticós.

Dorticós boasted, threatened, cajoled and did his best to make it appear that the uprising was the work of a "counter-revolutionary" minority and that it had been put down by a majority which was loyal to the regime. But he did not hesitate to remind his vast television audience that the stern counter-measures taken in Cárdenas were intended as a lesson to the rest of Cuba.

"This afternoon," he said, "has afforded a vigorous spectacle that demonstrates, on a single occasion, the force that sustains our revolution, and also serves as a warning to our enemies with this modest sample of the military strength of a people under arms. . . . Our enemies forget one fact: Revolutionaries are tempered and they grow in stature in struggle and combat. Our enemies forget that this is a revolution forged out of heroic efforts, and that we will always respond [with force] when faced with enemy aggressions. . . . If another provocation were to be tried here, the entire population of Cárdenas would respond with even more vigor and mettle!" (Here the Communists in the crowd set up the cry *"Paredón! Paredón!"*)

Dorticós admitted that things were far from rosy, but he blamed everything on the imperialists and counter-revolutionaries. "It is a fact," he said, "that we are facing difficulties and shortages. [But] in the first place, these shortages are a result of imperialist economic aggression. In the second place, the progressive increase in our people's consuming capacity has exceeded our present production capacity. It is also true that some of our mistakes and shortcomings have aggravated this situation. The enemy tries to take advantage of these material conditions, and uses them to promote popular discontent. . . .

"These shortages and sacrifices today are the price we must pay in order to attain tomorrow's abundance. We can overcome them only by our own work and our own efforts. Sacrifice tempers character, and we are a people accustomed to sacrifices. Workers and peasants, let us merge ourselves in a firm alliance! Let us construct the fatherland for workers and peasants! Let us smash, with the full weight of our revolutionary people, these parasites of the counter-revolution! . . . Do not allow these parasites to get away with another single act of provocation. We will not have to use these tanks or machine-guns on them. Your efforts alone are enough to crush them, comrades! If they repeat their provocations, then the people will crush them in the streets, or our armed forces will be here!"

Reports from various parts of the island indicate that most Cubans were shocked and horrified by the televised spectacle. Padre Humberto, who watched it in Santiago de Cuba, comments: "This was either an act of desperation or incredible stupidity on Castro's part. We in the underground, of course, were delighted, because the television show from Cárdenas only fanned the flames of the people's resentment. Why, for instance, had they chosen Cárdenas for this demonstration—Cárdenas, the historic 'Flag City' of Cuba, where the first banner of Cuban freedom was raised more than a century ago? Did Fidel Castro think that, in three years of terror, he had erased from our minds all pride in our historic past?"

Alonso León, the former soap salesman, now a seriously ill and prematurely old man living near Havana, watched the spectacle on television and was reminded of Hungary, a reaction which is mentioned by many Cubans. "The city of Cárdenas," he says, "was Cuba's 'Little Budapest'—less bloody, perhaps, but also not as final. Cuba's 'bloody Budapest' still may come."

## *The Kremlin Decides*

Moscow's displeasure with the political and economic bungling in the Castro regime became apparent in June 1962. Ambassador Sergei M. Kudryavtsev (who headed the Soviet spy ring in Canada which was exposed by Igor

Gouzenko in 1946) was summoned to the Kremlin for consultations. A week later, he was replaced by Russia's most trusted Cuban expert, Alexei Alekseyev, who came to Havana following the Mikoyan visit in February 1960.

Less than three weeks after the "Cárdenas uprising," Raúl Castro arrived in Moscow, accompanied by Ambassador Alekseyev, on a mission which marked the beginning of a new Soviet military build-up. Dr. José Ignacio Rasco, who has made a careful study of Russia's long-range plans to utilize Cuba as a western base from which to "export the revolution," believes that the Kremlin was motivated more by contempt for Castro than by sympathy or loyalty to a comrade who faced economic woes and problems of internal security.

"Instead of strengthening communism's beachhead in the western hemisphere," he says, "Castro, in the coldly calculating Kremlin view, had been guilty of economic bungling and infantile political behavior which was damaging Cuba's usefulness as a base for the subversion of Latin America. The Cuban regime was shaky, vulnerable, jeopardized by internal uprisings and rebellion. The Kremlin saw but one alternative—to take over its Caribbean axis-partner entirely and convert Cuba into a puppet state."

Raúl Castro's visit to Russia in July was followed a month later (August 27–September 2) by a much more impressive mission to Moscow headed by Ernesto (Ché) Guevara. Cuban underground observers attached particular significance to the fact that Guevara was accompanied by Comrade Emilio Aragonés, chief of personnel of the Cuban Armed Forces. Obviously, said these observers, "something concerning personnel as well as materiel is involved in these discussions."

A communiqué issued by the Kremlin on September 2, 1962, implied strongly that nothing more than "defensive measures" was under discussion. "During the stay in the

USSR of Ernesto Guevara Serna and Emilio Aragonés Navarro," the communiqué stated, "views were also exchanged about the threats of aggressive imperialist quarters with regard to Cuba. In view of these threats, the Government of Cuba addressed the Soviet Government with a request for help by delivering armaments and sending specialists for training Cuban servicemen.

"The Soviet Government attentively considered this request . . . and agreement was reached on this subject. As long as the above mentioned quarters continue to threaten Cuba, the Cuban Republic has every justification for taking necessary measures to insure its security and safeguard its sovereignty and independence, while all Cuba's true friends have every right to respond to this legitimate request."

However, even when this communiqué was issued, the new military build-up of Cuba was already well under way.

## *Operation Cuba: Phase Two*

Mariel, an excellent deep-water port on the northern coast of Pinar del Río province, received the first ships of the new Soviet armada in late July. People who lived near the docks were evacuated; then Russian guards were posted and Mariel became a restricted area. Cargoes were unloaded solely by Soviet personnel. But before these first ships sailed on their return voyage, the alert anti-Castro underground reported that this new "Soviet aid" operation was totally unlike any Cuba had seen before.

"During the month of August alone," one agent reported, "ten ships flying the Soviet flag and four others from Soviet-bloc countries landed troops and materiel in the restricted area of Mariel. The troops were largely Russian, and there were between 2,500 and 3,000 among the first arrivals. Within the next 60 days the number of

Soviet military personnel in Cuba was estimated to be between 15,000 and 20,000. On August 9, a ship of unknown nationality landed several hundred French-speaking Africans who wore their native attire. Slavic and African personnel both observed strict military discipline."

The ships continued to unload in Mariel; but during the month of September increased activity was reported in other ports—Bahía Honda, Havana, La Isabela de Sagua, Puerto Padre, Banes, Baracoa—on the northern coast, as well as at some ports along the southern coastline. The identifiable cargo included heavy artillery, antiaircraft guns, rocket launchers, electronic equipment, generators, heavy trailer-trucks, tractors, cement-mixers and earth-moving equipment.

"All Cuban troops and militia," an underground agent reported in September, "have been transferred from the garrisons along the [northern] coastal road and replaced by foreigners. The same seems to have been done on all other main routes over which materiel is moved from the ports to installations."

Nevertheless, the destinations of the major equipment and the character of the installations (confirmed later by official disclosures) were pinpointed with remarkable accuracy in many instances. Special activities were reported to be taking place on the San Antonio de los Baños air base, the largest in Cuba, which was declared out-of-bounds for Cubans in late August. Some 500 Russian and Czech pilots, engineers and maintenance men moved on to the base and began assembling the MIG fighters which began arriving early in September and what observers declared (correctly) were Ilyushin-28 bombers which were spotted later that month. Soviet construction teams were reported to be working on other air bases at San Julián, Cienfuegos, Santa Clara, Camagüey, Bayamo, and Holguín.

## *Concealed Weapons*

Early in September such active underground groups as the Students' Revolutionary Directorate (DRE) and the Unidad Revolucionaria (UR) produced alarming but convincing evidence that a critical factor in the Soviet build-up consisted of missiles of undetermined range, and the preparation of missile bases. The movement by night of long, canvas-covered objects, ranging from 60 to 100 feet in length, on trailer-trucks, was observed in Pinar del Río on the highway between Mariel and Guanajay, and in Las Villas province between the port of La Isabela and the city of Sagua la Grande. Descriptions of the size and configuration of these objects, as well as the type of trailers used to move them, were pieced together from a number of eyewitness reports. This fragmentary evidence indicated that they might be Soviet M-101 medium range missiles (known range 1,200 miles) similar to the U.S. Redstone. Tanker-trucks, of a type different from those used to transport gasoline, were believed to be carrying kerosene and liquid oxygen. Even more precise descriptions, sent out of Cuba late in August, established the presence of Soviet "Guideline" surface-to-air missiles (one of which brought down Francis Gary Powers' U-2), a fact which was quickly confirmed by U.S. intelligence.

However, the same Cuban sources also placed great stress on the amount of construction work that was going on, and particularly of below-surface installations. For example, one report compiled by the DRE in September stated: "We have evidence that missiles, rocket fuel, oxidizers, and other equipment are being stored underground in caves, tunnels and newly constructed installations below the surface. One of these strongholds, probably the largest in the island, is located in the Yumurí Valley, about a mile from the coast and approximately five miles from Matanzas city.

"Construction of this complex was started about 18 months ago; but since August the base has been under absolute Soviet control and is barred to all but a few authorized Cuban workers. However, this general description can be accepted as authentic and verified: In the northern end of the valley there are camouflaged runways, leading to a tunnel the mouth of which is 35 feet high and 70 feet wide. The length of the tunnel is unknown, but it is believed to extend under the Vía Blanca, the road which runs between the valley and the coast.

"Located in the southeastern area are the now inactive Margot mines, where tunnels have been enlarged and new tunnels constructed. Modern ventilation and new power plants have been installed. We have observed quantities of armaments, including what are believed to be missiles of medium and intermediate range, being transported to this installation, and stored underground. Nothing that enters this area, with the possible exception of the moving equipment, is later seen on the surface."

Submarine bases were reported under construction, one in Havana harbor, another at Banes in Oriente province. Unable to conceal the huge development within sight of Havana, Castro declared in September that this was to be a "port for the Soviet fishing industry." The anti-Castro underground came back with the statement that the development actually was a base for Russian submarines, and also added that a number of Golem II nuclear missiles, which can be launched from any surface vessel or surfaced submarines, were already in Cuba. (Presence of the Golem missiles was verified late in October.)

On September 21, 1962, the DRE passed along an observation attributed to a "western diplomat" stationed in Havana: "If the nations of the Western Hemisphere do not take military action against Castro immediately, or at least within the next few months, Cuba will possess bases armed with nuclear weapons capable of destroying the most strategic zones in the United States." While the work was being carried on secretly, he added, both Russians and Cubans were proceeding on the assumption that "the United States Government will go on believing that these military installations are purely defensive measures."

For almost 90 days, these reports from inside Cuba, plus much corroborative data collected by U.S. intelligence, were placed in the hands of key policy-makers in Washington. Officially, at least, the reports were downgraded or dismissed. On August 24, a State Department spokesman stated: "We have seen nothing of any military significance. The ships coming in during the last few weeks must be seen in the larger context of the Soviets' trying to keep Castro afloat."

Unofficially, there was a tendency to dismiss the reports contemptuously as "information from refugee sources." One knowledgeable Cuban, who has played a major role in evaluating Cuban information and channeling it to U.S. intelligence agencies, offers this comment: "Information from refugee sources is like all 'raw intelligence'—it may range from fantasy and falsehoods to hard facts, however fragmentary, which can be of enormous value in constructing a significant picture of a given situation. Moreover, in the case of Cuba, we bear in mind that Castro's people have been known to deliberately plant or 'leak' false information which then can be discredited to the detriment of the people who believed it and passed it on. We believe that we are mindful of all these pitfalls and deliberate traps and know how to avoid them. When the records of the Castro regime become available ultimately, we believe what some people call 'refugee reports' will prove to have been very accurate and revealing."

However, there was another aspect to the Washington situation. Sometime in August a report was prepared by a special subcommittee of the House Armed Services Committee; when this was finally released on September 19, it revealed decided awareness of what was going on in Cuba. "The Soviet build-up of a military capacity in Cuba continues at an increased tempo," the report stated. "The most modern jet-fighter aircraft appear in increasing numbers on Cuban airfields, and Soviet 'technicians' continue to arrive in increasing numbers, and there can be no assurance that this build-up does not forecast the establishment of a missile capacity in Cuba as a hostile threat to the United States."

### *The "Hard" Intelligence*

Actually, United States intelligence had not been idle or caught napping. Beginning in August, when the presence in Cuba of the Guideline surface-to-air missiles was confirmed, U.S. reconnaissance planes maintained constant surveillance of Soviet ships at sea as well as of the unloading and disposition of the cargoes in Cuba. Then, on September 5, a U-2 plane which had been loaned to the Chinese on Formosa was shot down over Red China. There are two versions of what happened thereafter. One version is that the U-2 flights over Cuba were temporarily suspended, because the high-altitude reconnaissance plane was vulnerable to attack from Soviet surface-to-air missiles now installed in Cuba, and were not resumed until October 14 after an additional delay caused by Hurricane Ella. The second version maintains that while the U-2 flights may have been suspended for a time, other types of U.S. aircraft maintained the regular reconnaissance of Cuba whenever weather permitted. Thus, during the critical six weeks between September 5 and October 14, the Soviet build-up in Cuba was still under the prying eyes of U.S. aerial intelligence. This version also emphasizes a point generally overlooked: thanks to the refugee reports and other information from inside Cuba, all U.S. reconnaissance flights knew exactly where to look and what to look for.

It was on October 14, however, that a U-2 flight brought back the photographs that completed the hard "before and after" evidence that the United States was seeking. Compared with earlier photographs of the same sites, the October 14 shots provided unquestionable evidence of the Soviet missile build-up. Launching sites for medium-range (1,200 miles) missiles, of which Cuba now had a known minimum of 40, capable of bringing nuclear destruction to Washington, D.C., Cape Canaveral, the Panama Canal, Mexico City and any sector of the southeastern United States, Central America and the Caribbean, were already operational. Work was being completed on additional "hardened sites" for the launching of intermediate-range (2,500 miles) missiles which would extend the striking range to include all U.S. cities, and the hemisphere as far north as Hudson Bay, and south to Lima, Perú. Four of the installations were located, exactly as reported by the Cuban underground, at Guanajay (about 15 miles from the port of Mariel) and San Cristóbal, both in Pinar del Río province, and at Sagua la Grande and Remedios in Las Villas.

Special "sequential" photographs, taken over several days, traced the movement of equipment, and the construction of control bunkers, launch pads, storage depots for warheads. The movement of convoys from point to point proved another contention made earlier by the Cubans: medium-range missiles were stored underground, to be transported to the launching pads as needed. Intermediate-range missiles were to be installed permanently on the "hardened" sites still under construction.

Ilyushin-28 bombers, with a range of 700 miles, and capable of carrying five-megaton bombs, were photographed crated, in various stages of assembly, and standing completely operational on the field. On the night of October 22, following the President's official disclosure on television of the missile build-up, Secretary of Defense Robert S. McNamara displayed to newsmen, in addition to evidence of the missile sites and their equipment, photographs of the IL-28 aircraft crated, as they were first sighted aboard Soviet ships at sea.

Asked if there were nuclear warheads in Cuba, Secretary McNamara replied: "We don't know. Nuclear warheads are of such a size that it is extremely unlikely that we would ever be able to observe them by the intelligence means open to us. I think it is almost inconceivable, however, that there would be missiles, as I have indicated, without accompanying warheads."

### *The Quarantine*

President John F. Kennedy, in a brief, somber address on the evening of October 22, 1962, exposed to the nation and the world the brazen Soviet deception which had converted Castro's Cuba into a nuclear missile-base under the absolute control of Russian personnel. "It shall be the policy of this nation," he said solemnly, "to regard any nuclear missile launched from Cuba against any nation of the Western Hemisphere as an attack by the Soviet Union on the United States requiring a full retaliatory response upon the Soviet Union." He also indicated that the United States would take steps immediately "to prevent the use of these missiles against this or any other country, and to secure their withdrawal or elimination from the Western Hemisphere." The first step was a quarantine—or blockade—to prevent any additional offensive weapons from reaching Cuba.

The naval and air blockade of Cuba went into effect on the morning of October 24. U.S. warships ranged over thousands of square miles of the Caribbean and patroled the sea lanes ready to turn back or board-and-search ships bound for Cuba. The air patrol over the high seas reported that, during the first twenty-four hours, Soviet ships, obviously Cuba bound, changed their courses or headed back to home ports. Russia, apparently, was unwilling to risk running the blockade or to submit highly secret cargoes to the scrutiny of U.S. boarding parties.

Meanwhile, the stepped up aerial reconnaissance of Cuba revealed that work on the intermediate-range missile sites was being speeded up instead of slowed down. Southern Florida became a vast staging area, and throughout the United States units of the Army, Air Force and Marines mobilized for the next step, which might be an invasion of Cuba, aerial bombardment of the missile sites, or both.

The crisis lasted until October 28 when an exchange of notes between Washington and Moscow ended with Khrushchev's capitulation. "Esteemed Mr. President," he wrote, "I regard with respect and trust your statement . . . of October 27, that no attack will be made on Cuba, that no invasion will take place. . . . In view of this, the motives which prompted us to give aid of this nature to Cuba are no longer applicable. Hence we have instructed our officers to take the necessary measures to stop the building of these objectives, dismantle them, and return them to the Soviet Union. As I have told you in my letter of October 27, we are ready to come to an agreement that representatives of the U.N. may verify the dismantling of these means. . . ."

However, it still was necessary to deal with the Kremlin's frustrated and irascible vassal, Fidel Castro, who said he would permit no on-site inspections, even under U.N. auspices. There was also the unresolved question of what to do about the IL-28 bombers, which Castro claimed were free gifts from the Soviet Union and therefore Cuban property which he refused to surrender.

In the end, Comrade Castro bowed to the will of his Soviet masters. First Deputy Premier Anastas I. Mikoyan flew to Havana for a "two-day conference" and remained there for weeks. But on November 20, President Kennedy was able to state at his televised press conference: "I have today been informed by Chairman Khrushchev that all the IL-28 bombers now in Cuba will be withdrawn within thirty days. He also agrees that these planes can be observed and counted [from the air] as they leave. Inasmuch as this goes a long way toward reducing the danger which faced this Hemisphere four weeks ago, I have this afternoon instructed the Secretary of Defense to lift our naval quarantine."

### *The Blighted Hopes*

Cubans-in-exile watched, with sorrow and resentment, as the crisis which they had hoped would bring about Cuba's liberation, ended in a compromise that provided no on-site inspections of what was still inside Castro's "Kremlin-West." One high officer of the anti-Castro movement, who cannot be named, had this to say:

"We think it would be more correct to describe the Cuban attitude as one of utter dismay. How can one accept, so soon after such brazen and carefully planned deception, the word of the Communist *responsables* that the military build-up of Castro's Cuba has been dissembled and withdrawn? Upon what authority do we base the assumption that the missiles and bombers, observed aboard ships coming out of Cuba, are all that were there? Do we now accept the word of Khrushchev, Castro, Mikoyan and others as the word of honorable men? What about the MIG fighters and the nuclear warheads which the U.S. government conceded were in Cuba—are they not there still? And is it not conceded by authorities on military aviation that racks for the carrying of nuclear bombs are easily attached to fighters of these MIG types. Finally, how about the identified and conceded underground storage depots and the caves with which Cuba is honeycombed? Is it not likely that these still harbor offensive weapons of the most dangerous types?

"We do not know what to make of the over-extended stay of Mikoyan in Cuba; but we cannot forget his past record as the monster of Hungary. We are unwilling, also, to believe that he spent all his time coaxing Castro to accede to Khrushchev's promise to retrieve the bombers. We think it is significant that, with the life-or-death power the Soviet Union has over Cuba's future, that Mikoyan was unable to get Castro to consent to any form of on-site inspection, even under the innocuous and doubtful auspices of the International Red Cross.

"Whether Mikoyan's prolonged visit resulted in any extended program of Soviet economic aid to Castro remains to be seen. However, if the Russians choose to subsidize Cuba for any prolonged period of time, it will be only because they still value the island as a beachhead in the hemisphere for exporting the Castro-Communist revolution to other nations in the Caribbean and on the continent. If that is the case, there will be other and more troublesome incidents in the future. We shall have to wait and see and, so far as we Cubans are concerned, we intend to increase rather than relax our vigilance."

Cuban claims that Castro's island was still the Soviet Union's base for exporting the revolution received surprising support in December from Khrushchev himself. Denying the charges of Red China and Albania that he had "capitulated to imperialism" by withdrawing Soviet missiles and bombers from Cuba, Khrushchev boasted: "Socialist Cuba exists. Cuba remains a beacon of Marxist-

Leninist ideas in the Western Hemisphere. The impact of the revolutionary example will grow. . . ."

Fire-breathing Ché Guevara went even further in an interview with a correspondent of the Communist *Daily Worker* of London. The article had to be toned down considerably before publication, but the United Press International obtained a copy of the unexpurgated text. Guevara promised that, with Cuba's help, the revolution would be duplicated successfully in all Latin American countries. He mentioned Venezuela, Guatemala, Paraguay, Perú, Colombia and Nicaragua specifically. "There is no other solution possible in these countries except armed struggle," he said. "The objective conditions for this exist, and Cuba's example has shown these countries the way."

But, in the same interview, Ché Guevara made an even more ominous statement. "If the rockets had remained," he said, "we would have used them all and directed them against the very heart of the United States, including New York."

## *The Bitter Lessons*

Christmas week 1962 in Miami was emblazoned by more than Yuletide decorations and bright skies. Beginning on Christmas Eve, the 1,113 men of Brigade 2506, who had been Fidel Castro's captives since April 1961, were returned to freedom in Florida, ransomed by some $60 million dollars worth of pharmaceuticals and foodstuffs, a partial expiation for the U.S. blunders in the Bay of Pigs tragedy.

To the last man, they were proud, undefeated warriors, who had resisted the evils of Communist brainwashing and survived the rigors and deprivations of Castro's jails. They were also firm in their determination to fight again for Cuba's freedom.

Manuel Artime, civilian leader of the Liberation Army, declared: "We will fight again. We have given our word to our dead, to the Cuban people, and to the Free World that we will liberate Cuba or die in the attempt."

On Saturday, December 29, 35,000 Cubans filled the grandstands of Miami's Orange Bowl as President Kennedy reviewed the officers and men of Brigade 2506 and accepted its proudest possession—the Brigade colors. "I want to express my great appreciation to the Brigade," the President said, "for making the United States the custodian of this flag. I can assure you that this flag will be returned to the Brigade in a free Havana."

Said José San Roman, commander of the Brigade: "We don't know how or in what form the opportunity will come for us to fight in the cause of Cuba. Whenever, however, wherever, in whatever honorable form it may come, we will do what we can to be better prepared to meet and complete our mission."

Liberation, to most Cubans, was only a matter of time. José Ignacio Rasco expressed the solemn, hopeful, long-range view. "We are aware," he said, "that our struggle will only begin with the liberation of Cuba. We will face enormous tasks in rebuilding our Communist-wrecked economy, in installing a new democratic government with democratic safeguards, and—perhaps the greatest task of all—in rehabilitating a generation of Cubans whose minds have been perverted by Communist indoctrination.

"We have learned some bitter lessons, and we have more to learn still. But I think the free people of the Western Hemisphere have much to learn with us, both from our sad experience and our future actions. The most solemn lesson, I believe, is this: Never again must the free people anywhere in the Americas say, as we said in Cuba, 'communism can never happen here.' "